scarfSTYLE

Innovative to traditional, 31 inspirational styles to knit and crochet

scarf STYLE

Innovative to traditional,
31 inspirational styles to
knit and crochet

PAM ALLEN | editor of INTERWEAVE KNITS

INTERWEAVE
interweavestore.com

ILLUSTRATIONS: **Ann Swanson and Gayle Ford**

PHOTOGRAPHY: **Carol Kaplan**

PHOTO STYLING: **Pam Allen and Jillfrances Gray**

DESIGN: **Jillfrances Gray**

INTERWEAVE PRESS LLC
201 East Fourth Street
Loveland, Colorado 80537 USA
interweavestore.com

PRINTED IN **Singapore by Tien Wah Press (Pte Limited)**

Library of Congress Cataloging-in-Publication Data

Allen, Pam, 1949–
Scarf style : innovative to traditional,
31 inspirational styles to knit and crochet / Pam Allen.
p. cm.
Includes bibliographical references and index.
ISBN 978-1-931499-54-5
1. Knitting–Patterns. 2. Crocheting–Patterns. 3. Scarves. I. Title.
TT825.A454 2004
746.43'20432–dc22
2004005546

15 14 13 12 11 10 9 8

ACKNOWLEDGMENTS

I am greatly indebted to the following for their contributions to this book:

Ann Budd, for proofing the patterns, putting together the glossary, and expertly turning a rambling design chapter into a succinct and cohesive whole.

Jillfrances Gray for her elegant book design and her invaluable contribution to the photostyling.

Photographer Carol Kaplan for the beautiful photographs that make the most of the scarves shown in this book.

Models Michael Hayes, Rebecca Gray, Rachel Davis, Frances Denny, Trinette Faint, Caitlin FitzGerald, and Joan FitzGerald Denny.

The proprietors of the Brattle Book Shop, Garden of Eden, and Nightingale Restaurant who allowed us to take pictures in their establishments and to the Boston Center for the Arts for the use of the Mills Gallery.

Roger Sterns and Joan FitzGerald Denny for welcoming us so warmly into their homes.

Stephen Beal for his infallible copyediting.

Lori Gayle for her expert tech editing—and her funny stories.

Betsy Armstrong, Linda Stark, and Linda Ligon for their willingness to listen, at length, to my ideas.

The yarn companies who graciously contributed the yarn to make the scarves.

The designers of the scarves in this book whose creative talents never fail to inspire me.

CONTENTS

Scarf Style is a book of scarves to knit and a book about knitting scarves.

WHY SCARVES?

A scarf on the needles is the comfort food of knitting. Whatever else we're working on, whatever else the day holds for us, we can return to the scarf we're making with a sense of pleasure and relief. A scarf allows us to forget about the rigors of gauge. A scarf always fits its wearer, whether it ends up an inch narrower or wider, shorter or longer than intended. Worked in a familiar pattern, a scarf is soothing to knit. If we decide to add random stripes here and there, or we use the scarf as a sampler of knitting patterns; if we change the stitch pattern halfway through, or knit the entire scarf in simple garter stitch: whatever we do becomes a coherent design by the time we bind off. And of course, scarves are a comfort in the wearing, wrapping us in soft, reassuring warmth. And what makes a better gift than a handknitted scarf?—a virtual hug to the recipient with our carefully constructed stitches.

To extend the food metaphor, knitting a scarf is a bit like making a favorite pasta dish. Like pasta, scarves can be created with little effort and a few basic materials. You can follow a knitting pattern or cooking recipe to the letter with excellent results. Yet both are good vehicles for creative elaboration. Depending on the techniques you use and the ingredients at hand, you can whip up basic weekday pasta or a dazzling gourmet treat. With yarn and needles, you can create any number of scarves depending on your mood, your time, your skill level, and what's in your stash. Yarn, needle size, stitch pattern, colors, even the direction you work, can be combined in endless ways to create wonderful scarves and satisfying knitting experiences.

Scarf Style is a book of scarves to knit and a book about knitting scarves. It's a collection of patterns (or recipes) for scarves collected from more than thirty knitwear designers, each of whom has interpreted the idea of a scarf in a particular way. Each scarf is

individual, yet together they represent the creative ingenuity of these designers and the myriad ways you can think about this most basic of garments. From a traditional scarf whose beauty lies in its timeless stitch patterns to a "scarf" that's really a pair of portable sleeves with a turtleneck, from a delicate triangular shawl based on nineteenth-century Estonian lace patterns to a "striped" scarf made from separate knitted strips held together with bobbles, the scarves in this book expand our idea of what a scarf can be. They give us new ways to think about this classic knitting project and, in the way the designers have explored the techniques of knitting to make them, they add to our understanding of creative knitting possibilities.

If you'd like to design your own scarf, turn to the Design Notebook on page 126. Whether you're new to knitting, or you've been knitting forever, this chapter can help you make an imaginative scarf that's simple or complex, sophisticated or whimsical. To get you started, you'll also find in the Designer's Notebook a template for a basic scarf, along with many suggestions for how to vary your design through stitch pattern and colorwork.

At the end of the book, you'll find a Glossary of terms and techniques as well as instructions for the basic mechanics of knitting. The simple directions and illustrations should provide all the help and reminders you'll need.

So set down your fork, and pick up your needles . . . a scarf awaits you.

The scarves in this book expand our idea of what a scarf can be.

scarfPATTERNS

Kristin Nicholas confesses that for her, knitting a scarf can be tedious. "It goes on and on forever and when you look down at your progress, you still have more to do." Devoted to knitting in the round, Kristin decided to use the length of her circular needle to help her out. She cast on the entire length of the scarf and began knitting. That way, she only had to knit eight inches to make a full-size scarf. Working a stripe pattern into the scarf added some visual interest and made the knitting part more fun. And no need to weave in the ends. They can be knotted and incorporated into the pom-poms.

SCARF

With MC, CO 260 sts. Knit 1 row on WS.

Rows 1–4: Knit.

Rows 5–8: Change to pink and knit 4 rows.

Rows 9–12: Change to MC and work 4 rows St st (knit on RS, purl on WS).

Rows 13–16: Change to green and knit 4 rows.

Rows 17–20: Change to MC and work 4 rows St st.

Rows 21–24: Change to rust and knit 4 rows.

Rows 25–28: Change to MC and work 4 rows St st.

Rows 29–32: Change to honey and knit 4 rows.

Rows 33–36: Change to MC and work 4 rows St st.

Rows 37–68: Rep Rows 5–36 once.

Rows 69–72: Rep Rows 5–8 once.

Rows 73–77: Change to MC and knit 5 rows.

BO as if to knit on next row.

FINISHING

Weave in loose ends. Block lightly. **Pom-poms**: Following directions on pom-pom maker, make 10 multicolor pom-poms. (Or see Glossary for directions on making pom-poms.) Change colors randomly as you wind so the pom-poms will have large spots of color, instead of appearing striped. You can also wind with two colors of yarn held together, changing colors often, for more mottled looking pom-poms. Sew five pom-poms to each short end of scarf, with a pom-pom at each corner, and the other three evenly spaced in between.

FINISHED SIZE
10" (25.5 cm) wide and 65" (165 cm) long, not including pom-poms.

YARN
Devon Yarns Julia (50% wool, 25% kid mohair, 25% alpaca; 93 yd [85 m]/50 g): #6086 velvet moss (MC), 5 skeins; #5084 zinnia pink, #2163 golden honey, #0178 harvest spice (rust), and #5185 spring green, 1 skein each. Yarn distributed by Great Yarns.

NEEDLES
Size 8 (5 mm): 36" (90-cm) or longer circular (cir). Adjust needle size if necessary to obtain the correct gauge.

NOTIONS
Tapestry needle; pom-pom maker (optional).

GAUGE
16 sts and 25½ rows = 4" (10 cm) in St st.

Ribbed patterns often appear in knitted scarves because they lie flat and are reversible. Here, Norah Gaughan uses ribs as the basis for a cable pattern that has no right or wrong side. The cables are worked as a repeating allover motif and are turned on alternate sides. This richly textured scarf looks fairly complicated, but it's easy to remember what to do once you get the hang of it. Norah recommends blocking the scarf to open up the pattern and show off the interplay of cables.

NOTE
- Because this pattern has an odd number of rows, the cable row will alternate between the "right" and "wrong" sides each time it is worked.

FINISHED SIZE
7½" (19 cm) wide and 72" (183 cm) long.

YARN
Reynolds Odyssey (100% Merino; 104 yd [95 m]/50 g): #408 light green mix, 8 balls. Yarn distributed by JCA, Inc.

NEEDLES
Size 7 (4.5 mm). Adjust needle size if necessary to obtain the correct gauge.

NOTIONS
Cable needle (cn); tapestry needle.

GAUGE
20 sts and 25 rows = 4" (10 cm) in St st.

SCARF

CO 74 sts. Work reversible cable patt as foll:

Rows 1–6: P1, *k3, p3; rep from * to last st, k1.

Row 7: *Sl 6 sts onto cn and hold in front, p1, k3, p1, sl last st from cn to left needle and purl it, (p1, k3, p1) from cn, p2, k3, p2; rep from * to last 2 sts, p1, k1.

Rep Rows 1–7 until piece measures about 72" (183 cm) from beg, ending with Row 5 of patt. BO all sts in patt on next row.

FINISHING

Weave in loose ends. Block gently, spreading out scarf slightly.

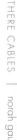

FORBES FOREST
KATHY ZIMMERMAN

The sylvan scenery of Pennsylvania's Forbes State Forest is the inspiration for Kathy Zimmerman's beautiful cable-stitch scarf. Kathy lives near the woods and has ample opportunity to study its features. The loden green color she's chosen, rich and earthy, reminds her of the lush undergrowth, the bobbles and frond cables suggest ferns and summer berries, and the curving zigzag stitches mimic the hiking trails as they wind their way deep into the woods.

STITCH GUIDE

Popcorn: ([K1f&b] 2 times, k1) in same st to make 5 sts, turn; p5; turn; ssk, k1, k2tog; slip second and third sts on right needle over the first st to dec back to 1 st.

Bobble: (K1, p1, k1) into same st to make 3 sts; turn; p3; turn; sl 2 sts as if to k2tog, k1, pass sl sts over to dec back to 1 st.

SCARF

CO 67 sts. **Set-up row:** (WS) K3 (edge sts, work in garter st throughout), place marker (pm), work center 61 sts according to set-up row from Forbes Forest chart, pm, k3 (edge sts, work in garter st throughout). Maintaining 3-st garter edges, rep Rows 1–20 of zigzag cables, and rep Rows 1–12 of frond cable (do not rep set-up row) until 420 patt rows have been completed (21 reps of zigzag cables; 35 reps of frond cable). BO all sts in patt.

FINISHING

Weave in loose ends. Block lightly.

FINISHED SIZE
8¾" (22 cm) wide and 61" (155 cm) long, after blocking.

YARN
Jaeger Matchmaker Merino Double Knitting (100% merino; 131 yd [120 m]/50 g): #890 seaweed, 5 balls. Yarn distributed by Westminster Fibers.

NEEDLES
Size 6 (4 mm). Adjust needle size if necessary to obtain the correct gauge.

NOTIONS
Markers (m); cable needle (cn); tapestry needle.

GAUGE
In zigzag cable panel, 21 sts = 2¾" (7 cm) wide and 27 rows = 4" (10 cm) high, after blocking; in frond cable panel, 19 sts = 2¼" (5.5 cm) wide and 27 rows = 4" (10 cm) high, after blocking.

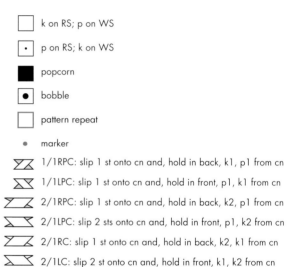

☐ k on RS; p on WS

• p on RS; k on WS

■ popcorn

⊙ bobble

☐ pattern repeat

• marker

⊠ 1/1RPC: slip 1 st onto cn and, hold in back, k1, p1 from cn

⊠ 1/1LPC: slip 1 st onto cn and, hold in front, p1, k1 from cn

⊠ 2/1RPC: slip 1 st onto cn and, hold in back, k2, p1 from cn

⊠ 2/1LPC: slip 2 sts onto cn and, hold in front, p1, k2 from cn

⊠ 2/1RC: slip 1 st onto cn and, hold in back, k2, k1 from cn

⊠ 2/1LC: slip 2 st onto cn and, hold in front, k1, k2 from cn

Forbes Forest

Left Zigzag Cable   Right Zigzag Cable

Front Cable

set-up row

Before Mags Kandis designed and made this scarf, she asked two friends for their thoughts on the perfect scarf. One said, "Lots of color patterns." The other said, "A yummy red, with cables and bobbles." She satisfied the wishes of both friends by using color patterns, an accent of red at the ends of the scarf (note the striped lining on the insides of the Fair Isle borders), and a lively combination of bobbles and cable patterns in the body. The unexpected combination of colorful patterns and cable texture remind Mags of a lively crazy quilt. Whimsical tassels, made with every color used in the scarf, finish off the ends.

STITCH GUIDE

Stripe Pattern: In St st, work the foll number of rows with each color: 5 raspberry, 3 purple, 2 charcoal, 3 gold, 3 green-gold, 2 raspberry, 2 pink, 10 raspberry, 2 purple, 2 pink, 3 charcoal, 2 gold, 4 green, 2 green-gold, 2 pink, 10 raspberry, 3 purple, 2 green, 2 charcoal, 3 gold, 5 raspberry.

SCARF

First striped lining: With raspberry, CO 56 sts. Beg with a RS (knit) row, work 72 rows of stripe pattern—piece should measure about 12" (30.5 cm) from beg. Change to pink and knit 1 row (RS), inc 5 sts evenly spaced—61 sts. Knit the next row (WS) for turning row. *First colorwork section*: Change to green-gold and beg with Row 1, work Rows 1–68 of Colorwork chart in stranded St st—piece should measure about 12" (30.5 cm) from turning row. Change to charcoal and knit 1 row. *Next row*: (WS) K2tog, knit to last 2 sts, k2tog—59 sts rem. *Cable section*: Change to raspberry and beg with Row 1, work Rows 1–24 of Cable chart 7 times, then work Row 1 once more—169 cable patt rows completed; cable section should measure about 29½" (75 cm); piece should measure about 42" (106.5 cm) from turning row, including first charcoal garter ridge. *Next row*: (WS) K4, purl to last 4 sts, k4. Change to charcoal and knit 2 rows, inc 1 st each end of needle on last row—61 sts. *Second colorwork section*: Change to green-gold and raspberry. Turn Colorwork chart upside down, and work in rev order, from Row 68 to Row 1. *Second striped lining*: Change to pink and knit 1 row (RS), dec 5 sts evenly spaced—56 sts rem. Knit the next row (WS) for turning row. Work 72 rows of stripe pattern in rev order (beg with 5 raspberry, 3 gold, and end with 3 purple, 5 raspberry). BO all sts.

FINISHED SIZE
12" (30.5 cm) wide and 54½" (138.5 cm) long, not including tassels.

YARN
Mission Falls 1824 Wool (100% superwash Merino; 85 yd [78 m]/50 g): #029 raspberry (MC), 5 skeins; #014 Dijon (green-gold), #013 curry (gold), #025 mallow (pink), #004 charcoal, #028 pistachio (green), #023 amethyst (purple), 1 skein each. Yarn distributed by Unique Kolours.

NEEDLES
Size 8 (5 mm). Adjust needle size if necessary to obtain the correct gauge.

NOTIONS
Cable needle (cn); tapestry needle.

GAUGE
18 sts and 24 rows = 4" (10 cm) in St st; 20 sts and 22 rows = 4" (10 cm) in charted colorwork patt; 20 sts and 23 rows = 4" (10 cm) in charted cable patt.

FINISHING

Weave in loose ends. Fold scarf along turning rows with WS tog, and align BO and CO edges with charcoal ridges at each end. With yarn threaded on a tapestry needle, sew lining side seams. Slip-stitch linings closed along top edges on WS. *Tassels*: Cut fourteen 5" (12.5-cm) strands of each color. Using 7 strands in each tassel (1 each of the 7 colors), make fourteen fat 2" (5-cm) tassels (see Glossary), using random-colored scraps to wrap the "neck" of each tassel. With green, attach 7 tassels to the turning row at each end of the scarf. Block lightly to even out the colorwork and texture patterns.

☐	cable chart: k on RS; p on WS	1/1RT:	knit the second st on left needle, then knit the first st, then sl both sts off together
•	cable chart: p on RS; k on WS	2/1RPC:	sl 1 st onto cn and hold in back, k2, p1 from cn
▨	raspberry	2/1LPC:	sl 2 sts onto cn and hold in front, p1, k2 from cn
−	green-gold	2/1/2RC:	sl 3 sts onto cn and hold in back, k2, sl purl st from cn back on left needle and purl it, k2 from cn
+	gold		
○	pink		
■	charcoal	● bobble:	(K1, yo, k1, yo, k1) all in same st, turn, p5, turn, k5, turn, p2tog, p1, p2tog, turn, sl 1 st, k2tog, pass slipped st over
⁄	green		
I	purple		

Cable

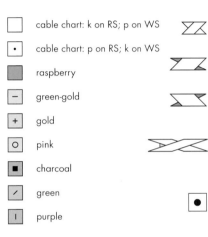

23
21
19
17
15
13
11
9
7
5
3
1

Colorwork

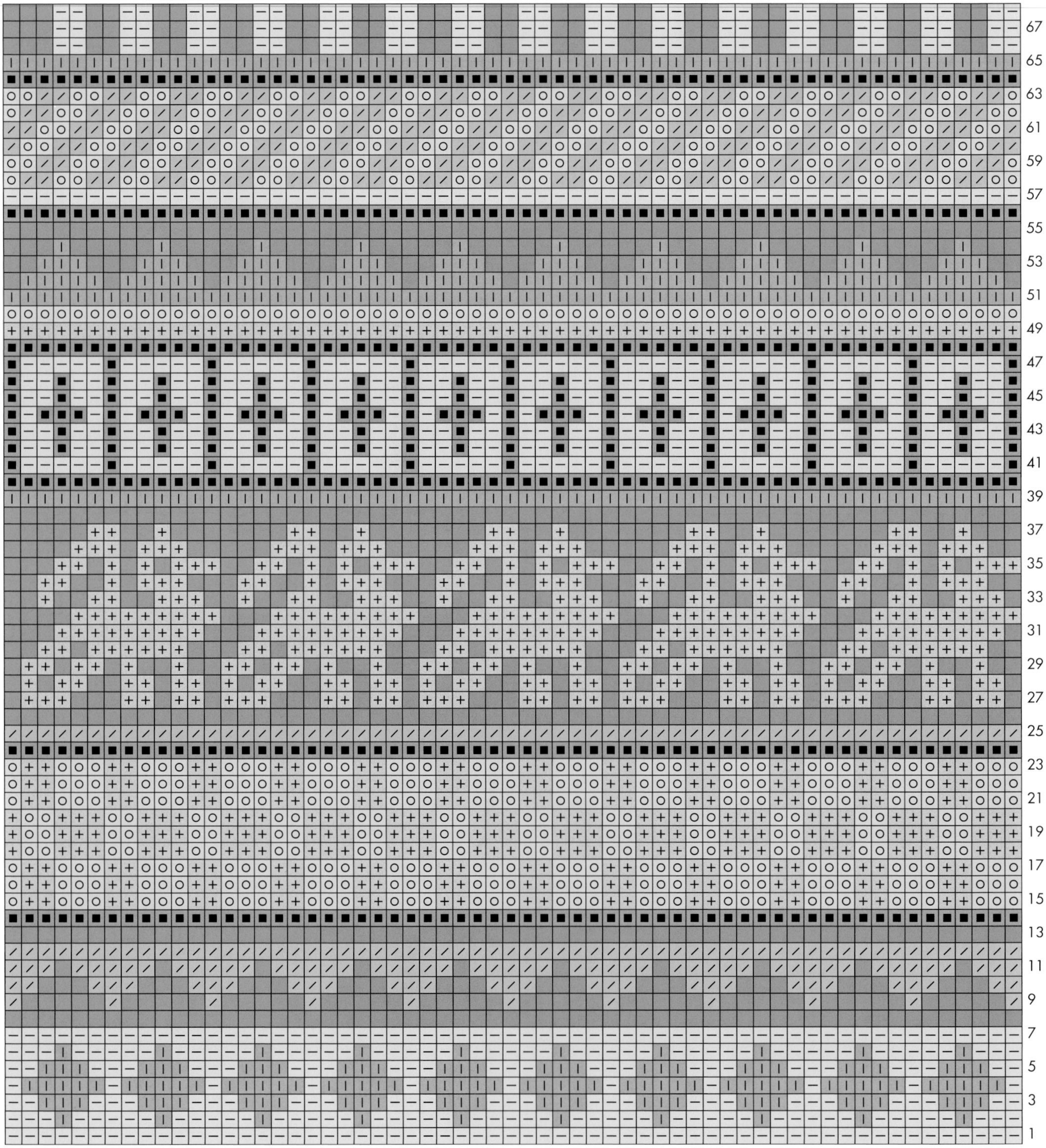

Teva Durham likes to find ways to rethink traditional knitting patterns. Here she's taken an Aran classic, the braided or woven cable, and used it as an allover pattern for a scarf. The dramatic, costume feel of intertwining cables that resemble plaited hair or Celtic metalwork have particular appeal for Teva, and she's worked the scarf in a soft, felted tweed yarn. The little patches of accent color give the scarf, in Teva's words, a "ragamuffin" feel, as if the scarf had a long history and had been darned on more than one occasion.

STITCH GUIDE

Braided Cable: (multiple of 6 sts)
Row 1: (RS) *Sl 3 sts onto cn and hold in front, k3, k3 from cn; rep from *.
Rows 2, 4, and 6: Purl.
Rows 3 and 7: Knit.
Row 5: K3, *sl 3 sts onto cn and hold in back, k3, k3 from cn; rep from * to last 3 sts, end k3.
Row 8: Purl.
Repeat Rows 1–8 for pattern.

> **NOTE**
> ❖ Felted Tweed colors are doubled throughout. Rowanspun DK colors are worked with a single strand.

SCARF

With MC doubled and using the Continental method (see Glossary), CO 30 sts. Purl 1 row. Beg with Row 1, work braided cable patt, introducing random patches of accent colors as foll: On Row 2 or Row 6 of braided cable patt, join accent color to the 1st, 4th, 7th, 10th, 13th, 16th, 19th, 22nd, 25th, or 28th st from beg of row (see Note about which colors to use double or single). Cont in patt for 6 rows, working 3 sts in the accent color, and stranding the MC loosely behind the work. When 6 rows have been completed, break off accent color

FINISHED SIZE
5¾" (14.5 cm) wide and 66" (167.5 cm) long, including fringe tabs.

YARN
Rowan Felted Tweed (50% Merino, 25% alpaca, 25% viscose rayon; 189 yd [173 m]/50 g): #147 dragon (gray-green, MC), 4 balls (used double); #139 crush (purple) and #141 whisper (teal), 1 ball each. Rowan Rowanspun DK (100% wool; 218 yd [200 m]/50 g): #747 catkin (light green) and #731 punch (orange), 1 ball each. Yarn distributed by Westminster Fibers.

NEEDLES
Size 10½ (6.5 mm). Adjust needle size if necessary to obtain the correct gauge.

NOTIONS
Cable needle (cn); tapestry needle.

GAUGE
21 sts and 20 rows = 4" (10 cm) in cable pattern, with MC doubled.

and cont in MC until the next place where you want an accent patch to appear. Alternate accent colors and their placement according to your liking. Work until piece measures 64" (162.5 cm) or 2" (5 cm) less than desired length, ending with Row 1 or Row 5 of patt. BO all sts pwise.

FRINGE TABS

With MC or accent color (double or single as appropriate) and RS facing, pick up and knit the first 3 sts of CO edge. *Turn, p3, turn, k3, turn, p3, turn, BO all sts.* With MC or accent color as desired, pick up and knit the next 3 sts of the CO edge and rep from * to *. Cont working randomly colored fringe tabs in this manner across the entire CO edge; you will have five fringe tabs that point right, and five that point left. Work fringe tabs across the BO edge the same way.

FINISHING

Weave in loose ends. Lightly steam-block, being careful not to flatten the cables.

In this modern unisex scarf, Fiona Ellis combines symmetry and asymmetry, textured stitch pattern, and colorwork. She used a simple repeat of irregular colored stripes in an easy-to-remember "plaid" knit-and-purl stitch pattern. The stitch pattern alternates at regular intervals which makes the scarf reversible. She's used classic school colors—gray, blue, gold, deep red—and has knitted extra rows to make a scarf long enough to wrap several times around the neck.

SCARF

With gray, CO 42 sts. Knit 4 rows. Work plaid patt as foll:

Row 1: (RS) Change to light green. K2, p4, [k2, p2, k2, p6] 2 times, k2, p2, k2, p4, k2.

Row 2: *K6, p2, k2, p2; rep from * 2 more times, k6.

Rows 3–6: Rep Rows 1 and 2 two times.

Rows 7 and 8: Change to gold. Rep Rows 1 and 2.

Rows 9–12: Change to light green. Rep Rows 1 and 2 two times.

Row 13: Change to dark green. *K6, p2, k2, p2; rep from * 2 more times, k6.

Row 14: K2, p4, [k2, p2, k2, p6] 2 times, k2, p2, k2, p4, k2.

Rows 15–18: Rep Rows 13 and 14 two times.

Rows 19 and 20: Change to burgundy. Rep Rows 13 and 14.

Rows 21–24: Change to dark green. Rep Rows 13 and 14 two times.

Rows 25–30: Change to gray. Rep Rows 1 and 2 three times.

Rows 31 and 32: Change to med blue. Rep Rows 1 and 2.

Rows 33–36: Change to gray. Rep Rows 1 and 2 two times.

Rows 37–42: Change to light green. Rep Rows 13 and 14 three times.

Rows 43 and 44: Change to gold. Rep Rows 13 and 14.

Rows 45–48: Change to light green. Rep Rows 13 and 14 two times.

Rows 49–54: Change to dark green. Rep Rows 1 and 2 three times.

Rows 55 and 56: Change to burgundy. Rep Rows 1 and 2.

Rows 57–60: Change to dark green. Rep Rows 1 and 2 two times.

Rows 61–66: Change to gray. Rep Rows 13 and 14 three times.

Row 67 and 68: Change to med blue. Rep Rows 13 and 14.

Rows 69–72: Change to gray. Rep Rows 13 and 14 two times.

FINISHED SIZE
8" (20.5 cm) wide and 85" (216 cm) long, after blocking.

YARN
Mission Falls 1824 Wool (100% superwash Merino; 85 yd [78 m]/50 g): #015 putty (gray), #016 thyme (light green), and #017 heath (dark green), 2 skeins each; #010 russet (burgundy), #013 curry (gold), and #020 cornflower (med blue), 1 skein each. Yarn distributed by Unique Kolours.

NEEDLES
Size 7 (4.5 mm). Adjust needle size if necessary to obtain the correct gauge.

NOTIONS
Tapestry needle.

GAUGE
21 sts and 25 rows = 4" (10 cm) in pattern st.

Rep Rows 1–72 a total of 7 times, then work Rows 1–24 once more—piece should measure about 84½" (214.5 cm) from beg. Change to gray. Knit 4 rows. BO all sts kwise.

FINISHING

Weave in loose ends. Block lightly.

A knit-and-purl stitch pattern is a good choice for a reversible scarf.

Nancy Bush named her scarf in honor of her Estonian friend Ene Sokk. Nancy traveled to Estonia with Ene and her family in November of 2002 and remembers enjoying the hours she spent walking on snowy cobblestone streets where a warm scarf such as this one would have come in handy. Nancy's triangular scarf is based on traditional shawls from the seaside town of Haapsalu where local women have been knitting lace garments from sheep's wool since the early nineteenth century. While Nancy worked on her shawl, she listened to recordings of Estonian choir music and folk songs.

The shawl is worked by casting on for the two sides and worked to the center of the top edge. Four decreases are made on every decrease row; two are made just inside the border on the outer edges of the triangle, and a double decrease is worked along the center axis.

NOTES

❖ This scarf is cast on along the lower two sides and then decreased as it is worked upwards to the center of the top edge.

❖ The sections of the scarf inside the border markers have four decreases on every RS row (one decrease inside each border marker, and a double decrease centered in the middle of the scarf). Rows 23, 27, and 31 of Chart 2 are exceptions to this rule, and have six decreases each. Rows 23 and 31 have an extra single decrease just inside each border, and Row 27 has an extra k2tog on either side of center that is not paired with a yarnover. Row 179 of Chart 4 has only the centered double decrease.

❖ If desired, you may change to a shorter circular needle (optional) as the number of stitches decreases.

SCARF

With two strands of yarn held tog, and using the knitted method (see Glossary), CO 375 sts. Drop one of the strands and cont using a single strand of yarn throughout. Work Rows 1–22 from right and left halves of Chart 1, placing markers (pm) for the borders as indicated, and placing a coilless pin or removable stitch marker in the center st (move this pin up as the work progresses).

FINISHED SIZE

About 32" (81.5 cm) from bottom of point to top edge, measured straight up the center, 56" (142 cm) across the top edge, and 40" (101.5 cm) from bottom of point to top edge, measured along the side, before blocking.

YARN

Blackberry Ridge Lace Weight Silk Blend (75% wool, 25% silk; 350 yd [320 m]/ 2 oz [57] g): willow, 2 skeins.

NEEDLES

Size 6 (4 mm): 32" (80-cm) or longer circular (cir). Adjust needle size if necessary to obtain the correct gauge.

NOTIONS

Markers (m); tapestry needle; coilless safety pin or removable marker; 2 double-pointed needles (dpn) the same size or smaller than the main needles for working three-needle bind-off.

GAUGE

11 sts and 18 rows = 2" (5 cm) in St st.

Note: The center section of the scarf will dec by 4 sts every RS row, each border section will inc 1 st every other row four times, until there are eight border sts at each side. There will be 339 sts when Row 22 of Chart 1 has been completed. Change to Chart 2 and work Rows 23 to 32—313 sts. Change to Chart 3 and work Rows 33 to 56 once—265 sts. For Rows 57 to 152, rep Rows 33 to 56 four more times—73 sts rem. Change to Chart 4 and work Rows 153 to 179 once—19 sts rem (the center st and 9 sts at each side). Work the next WS row as foll: K2tog, yo, k7, k2tog, k8—18 sts rem. Arrange sts 9 each on two dpn and hold with RS tog. With the main needle and using the three-needle method (see Glossary), BO the two groups of sts tog.

FINISHING

Pin scarf out to desired shape, taking care to pin out the points along the CO edge. Place a damp towel over the scarf to block. When dry, weave in loose ends.

Chart 1, right half

Chart 1, left half

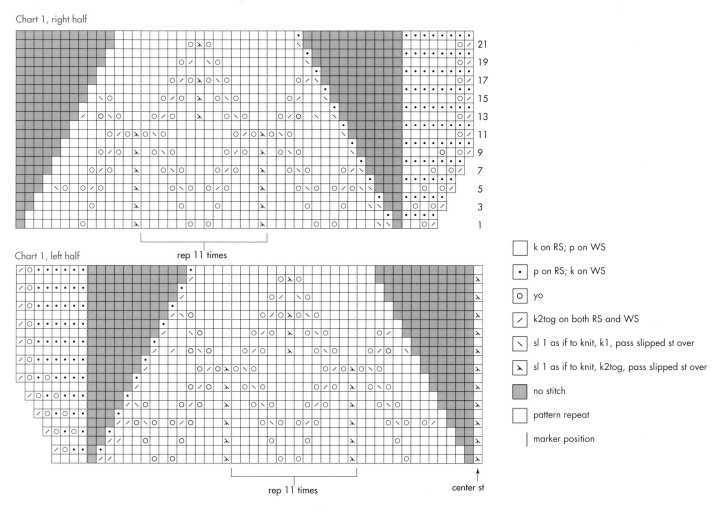

rep 11 times

rep 11 times

center st

☐	k on RS; p on WS
•	p on RS; k on WS
O	yo
╱	k2tog on both RS and WS
╲	sl 1 as if to knit, k1, pass slipped st over
⅄	sl 1 as if to knit, k2tog, pass slipped st over
(gray)	no stitch
☐	pattern repeat
│	marker position

Chart 2

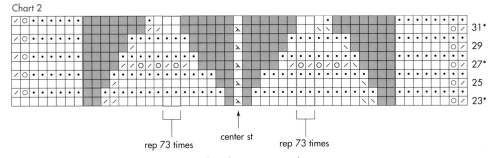

31*
29
27*
25
23*

rep 73 times   center st   rep 73 times

*Rows 23, 27, and 31 decrease 6 sts each; see Notes.

Chart 3

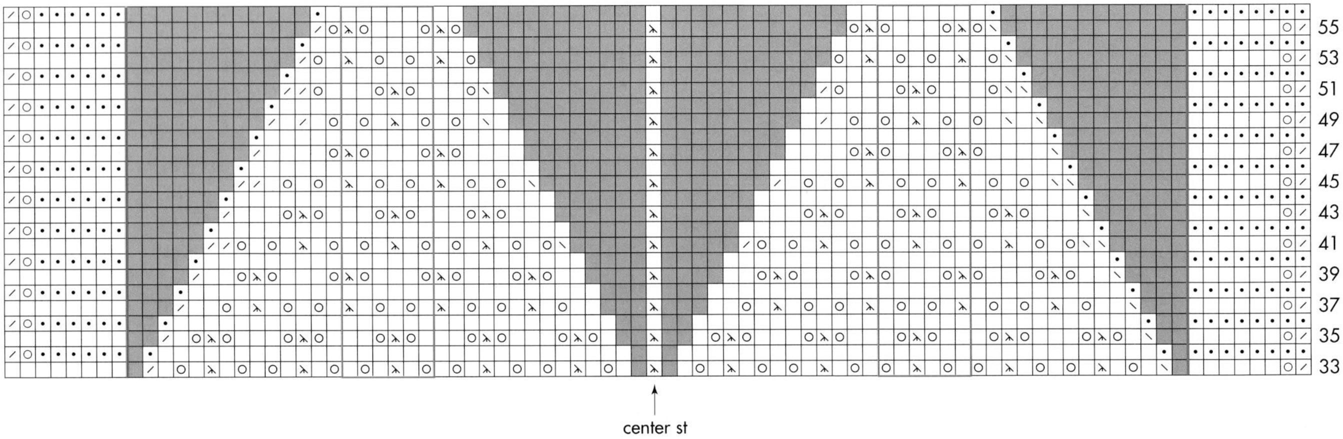

55
53
51
49
47
45
43
41
39
37
35
33

center st

Chart 4

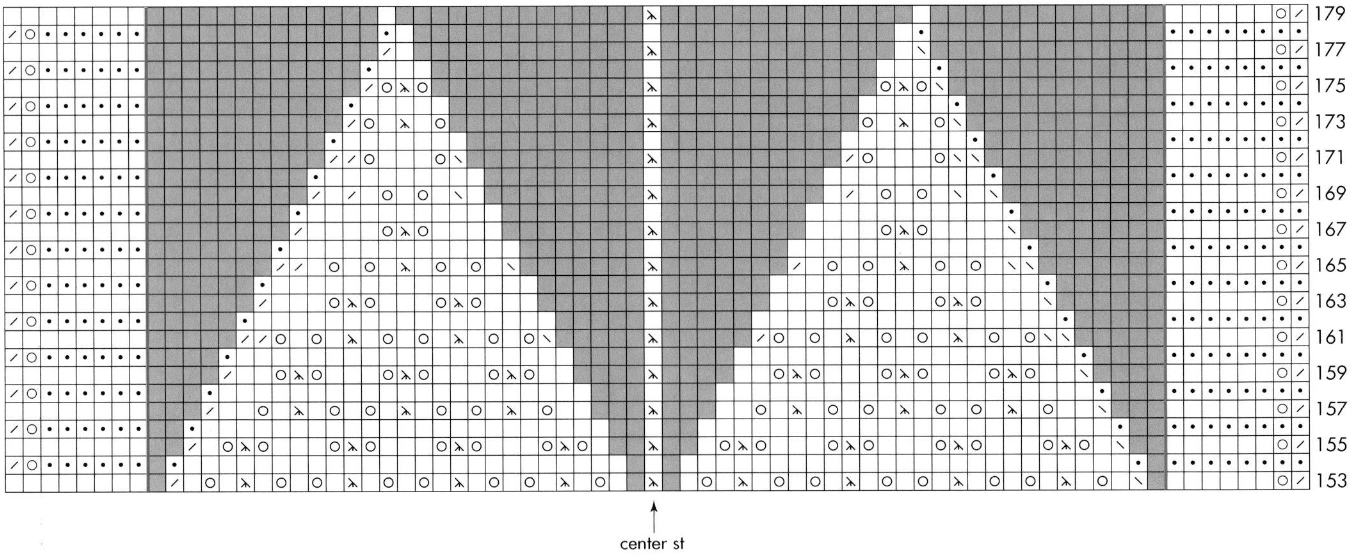

179
177
175
173
171
169
167
165
163
161
159
157
155
153

center st

Simple stripe patterns offer many design possibilities. In these vibrant blue and green scarves, Debbie Bliss has turned classic stripes into zigzags by working them in a chevron pattern. She likes the way the combination of strong colors and zigzags hark back to the jazzy patterns of the 1970s. Pom-poms on the border of the smaller scarf call attention to the funky, pointed ends.

STITCH GUIDE

Chevron Pattern:

Row 1: (RS) K1, ssk, *k9, sl 2 sts individually pwise, k1, p2sso; rep from * to last 12 sts, k9, k2tog, k1.

Row 2: K1, *p1, k4, (k1, yo, k1) all in next st, k4; rep from * to last 2 sts, p1, k1.

Repeat Rows 1 and 2 for pattern.

ADULT SCARF

With navy, CO 51 sts. Knit 1 row. Beg with Row 1, work chevron patt, changing colors according to the foll stripe sequence: 6 rows bright blue, 6 rows duck-egg blue, 6 rows apple green, 2 rows acid yellow, 6 rows dark green, 6 rows navy—32 rows total. Rep this 32-row stripe sequence until scarf measures about 72" (183 cm) from beg, ending with 6 rows of dark green. Change to navy and work Row 1 of chevron patt. With navy, BO all sts kwise.

FINISHING

Weave in loose ends. Block lightly, if desired.

FINISHED SIZE
Adult scarf measures 6" (15 cm) wide and 72" (183 cm) long; child's scarf measures 4½" (11.5 cm) wide and 38" (96.5 cm) long, not including pom-poms.

YARN
Debbie Bliss Merino DK (100% Merino; 122 yd [112 m]/50 g): Adult scarf: #214 navy, #202 bright blue, #203 duck-egg blue, #502 apple green, #503 acid yellow, #506 dark green, 1 ball each. Child's scarf: #506 dark green, 2 balls; #214 navy, #202 bright blue, #203 duck egg blue, #502 apple green, #503 acid yellow, 1 ball each. Yarn distributed by Knitting Fever, Inc.

NEEDLES
Size 7 (4.5 mm). Adjust needle size if necessary to obtain the correct gauge.

NOTIONS
Tapestry needle; cardboard or pom-pom maker for child's version.

GAUGE
34 sts and 26 rows = 4" (10 cm) in chevron patt.

CHILD'S SCARF

With navy, CO 39 sts. Knit 1 row. Beg with Row 1, work chevron patt, changing colors according to the foll stripe sequence: *2 rows bright blue, 2 rows duck-egg blue, 2 rows apple green, 2 rows acid yellow,* 2 rows dark green, 2 rows navy; rep from * to * once more. Change to dark green and work in chevron patt without stripes until piece measures about 34½" (87.5 cm), ending with Row 2 of patt. Cont in chevron patt, changing colors according to the foll stripe sequence: **2 rows acid yellow, 2 rows apple green, 2 rows duck-egg blue, 2 rows bright blue,** 2 rows navy, 2 rows dark green; rep from ** to ** once more. Change to navy and work Row 1 of chevron patt. With navy, BO all sts kwise.

FINISHING

Weave in loose ends. Block lightly, if desired. Make seven pom-poms (see Glossary), two each in apple green, acid yellow, and bright blue, and 1 in duck-egg blue. Attach three pom-poms to the points at one end of scarf, and four pom-poms to points at the other end.

A simple stripe repeat worked in a chevron stitch becomes a vibrant pattern.

NASTY DOG DRAGON SCARF
NICKY EPSTEIN

Nicky Epstein came up with her idea for a dragon scarf while watching a parade celebrating the Chinese New Year. As she watched an assortment of colorful dragons bobbing slowly down the street, she noticed a huge, doglike dragon that stopped to bestow blessings and to ward off evil spirits. To put up a barrier to cold winds, Nicky has given her knitted dragon the rich, warm hues of tangerine, lime, and cherry, and she's lined the scarf with a silk panel to prevent the long edges from rolling in. Once you've completed the dragon, the remainder of the scarf is worked in a tailored seed-and-stockinette stitch pattern. Nicky uses an ingenious method to create an off-beat fringe; it's worked from side-to-side by casting on and binding off for each strand.

SCARF

With MC, CO 57 sts. Knit 1 row, purl 1 row. Beg with Row 1 of Dragon Chart 1 (RS), work in patt using a separate length of yarn for each color motif, and crossing yarns at the color changes to avoid leaving holes. On Row 108, begin introducing seed st columns as shown on chart. When Row 126 of Chart 1 has been completed, change to Dragon Chart 2, and rep Rows 1 and 2 until piece measures 49" (124.5 cm) from beg, or 5" (12.5 cm) less than desired length, not including fringe. Work Rows 3–36 of Chart 2 once. Change to MC and knit 1 row, purl 1 row. BO all sts.

FINISHING

Weave in loose ends. Block lightly. *Fringe*: (Make two) With MC, make a slipknot and place it on the needle. *CO 9 sts (10 sts on needle), turn work and BO 9 sts; rep from * until piece meas 11" (28 cm) from beg (about 43 fringes). **Note**: Fringe will corkscrew while knitting. Steam-block the fringes to straighten, untwisting them carefully to avoid burning your fingers. *Lining*: Cut lining fabric to 2" (5 cm) longer than the finished scarf. Fold under 1" (2.5 cm) on all four sides of lining and press in place. With sewing needle and thread, sew lining to scarf all the way around. Using yarn threaded on a tapestry needle, sew fringes to the CO and BO edges at each short end.

FINISHED SIZE
11" (28 cm) wide and 54" (137 cm) long, not including fringe.

YARN
Jamieson's Shetland DK (100% wool; 150 yd [137 m]/2 oz [57 g]): #236 rosewood (MC, dark blue heather), 3 skeins; #478 amber (orange), #1200 nutmeg (rust), #587 madder (dark red), #1190 burnt umber (medium brown), #230 yellow ochre (gold), #1160 scotch broom (yellow), #250 leprechaun (medium green), and #147 moss (dark green), 1 skein each. Yarn distributed by Unicorn.

NEEDLES
Size 4 (3.5 mm). Adjust needle size if necessary to obtain the correct gauge.

NOTIONS
Tapestry needle; 13" (33-cm) piece of coordinating 60" (152.5-cm) wide dark plaid or Chinese silk lining fabric; matching thread and sharp-pointed sewing needle to attach lining.

GAUGE
20 sts and 29 rows = 4" (10 cm) in St st intarsia.

Dragon Chart 1

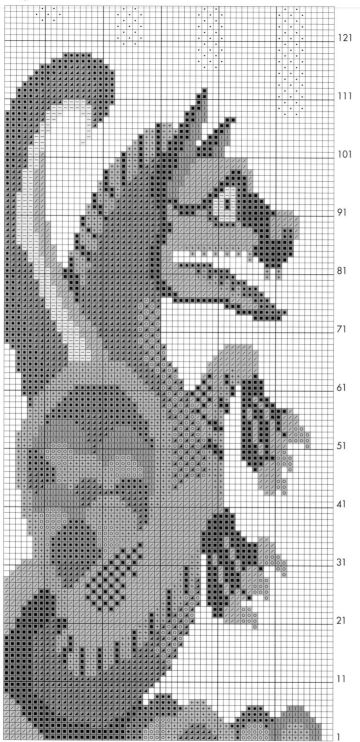

121
111
101
91
81
71
61
51
41
31
21
11
1

	MC: k on RS; p on WS
·	MC: p on RS; k on WS
−	yellow
+	orange
I	rust
O	gold
◢	medium brown
●	dark red
╱	medium green
■	dark green
	pattern repeat

Dragon Chart 2

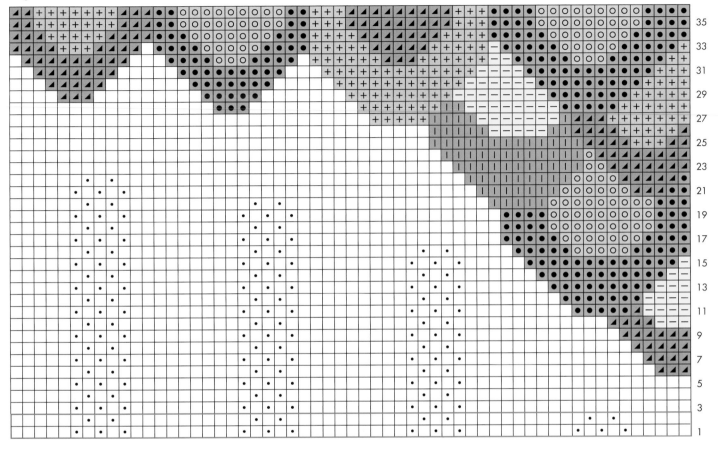

When working the intarsia motif, cut lengths of yarn about 36" long and let them dangle as you work. There's no need to wind them on separate bobbins.

INTERLOCKING BALLOONS
SHIRLEY PADEN

This scarf takes its undulating shape from an unusual cable-stitch pattern. After the cable crosses, the cable stitches separate into strands that flow out and back in again for the next cable crossing. Arranged in an interlocking series, the pattern resembles a graceful fleet of hot air balloons. Shirley Paden has made the scarf in a classic camel-colored yarn, a soft blend of Merino, alpaca, and silk. Try it in a bright mohair or shiny rayon for a very different effect.

STITCH GUIDE

M1R: Insert the left needle tip under the strand between the needles from front to back. Purl the lifted strand through the back loop to increase 1 stitch.

SCARF

CO 61 sts.

Row 1: (RS) *K1, p1; rep from *, end k1.
Row 2: *P1, k1; rep from *, end p1.
Next row: (RS) Knit. *Next row:* Establish selvedge sts and set up Balloon Stitch chart as foll: K1 (selvedge st), work center 59 sts according to set-up row 1 of chart, k1 (selvedge st). Cont to knit selvedge sts every row as established, work set-up rows 2 and 3 once, then work Rows 1–44 of patt 9 times (do not rep the set-up rows), then work Rows 1–42 once more. Knit 1 row (RS). *Next row:* *P1, k1; rep from *, end p1. *Next row:* *K1, p1; rep from *, end k1. BO all sts in rib patt.

FINISHING

Weave in loose ends. Block to finished measurements.

FINISHED SIZE:
9" (23 cm) wide and 62" (157.5 cm) long, after blocking.

YARN:
Maine Merino Marvelous Millennium Sportweight (75% Merino, 20% alpaca, 5% silk; 175 yd [160 m]/4 oz [114 g]): wallaby brown, 2 skeins.

NEEDLES:
Size 6 (4 mm). Adjust needle size if necessary to obtain the correct gauge.

NOTIONS:
Cable needle (cn); tapestry needle.

GAUGE:
30 sts = 4½" (11.5 cm) wide and 44 rows = 6" (15 cm) high in balloon st patt, after blocking.

Balloon Stitch

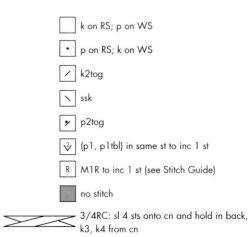

43
41
39
37
35
33
31
29
27
25
23
21
19
17
15
13
11
9
7
5
3
1

set-up row 3
set-up row 1

set-up row 2

☐	k on RS; p on WS
•	p on RS; k on WS
╱	k2tog
╲	ssk
⅄	p2tog
⅄̌	(p1, p1tbl) in same st to inc 1 st
R	M1R to inc 1 st (see Stitch Guide)
▨	no stitch
⨯⨯	3/4RC: sl 4 sts onto cn and hold in back, k3, k4 from cn

Amanda Blair Brown has created a striped scarf like no other. The stripes are worked as individual panels in a variety of tweed yarns, then connected by bright bobbles. Original and whimsical, this scarf makes a great beginner's project—knit and purl is all you need to do. And if your stripes come out a little longer or shorter than they're supposed to, it won't make a whit of difference.

STITCH GUIDE

K1, P1 Rib with Edge Stitches: (even number of sts)
All Rows: Sl 1 st knitwise with yarn in back (wyib), *p1, k1; rep from * to last st, p1.

Knot: Thread a 20" (51-cm) strand of either lime or fuchsia as indicated on a tapestry needle. Insert the needle into the edge of one strip and pull yarn through, leaving a 3" (7.5-cm) tail. Insert the needle into the edge of the adjacent strip, and knot the tail and the working yarn together to secure. With the working end of the yarn, pass the needle through the knotted circle and over a finger, pencil, or large knitting needle six times to form six loops. Flip the scarf over and form another set of six loops on the opposite side of the work. Make a couple of stitches through the base of all the loops. Tie the tail and working yarn tog again, and trim the ends very close to the knot.

STRIP 1
With medium gray, CO 8 sts. Work k1, p1 rib with edge stitches (see Stitch Guide) until piece measures 21" (53.5 cm) from beg. Change to violet and cont in patt until piece meas 53" (134.5 cm) from beg. Change to mustard and cont in patt until piece meas 84" (213.5 cm) from beg. BO all sts.

STRIP 2
With blackberry, CO 10 sts. Work k1, p1 rib with edge stitches until piece measures 21" (53.5 cm) from beg. Change to violet and cont in patt until piece meas 57" (145 cm) from beg. Change to dark green and cont in patt until piece meas 84" (213.5 cm) from beg. BO all sts.

FINISHED SIZE
4½" (11.5 cm) wide and 92" (233.5 cm) long.

YARN
Tahki Donegal Tweed Homespun (100% wool; 183 yd [167 m]/100 g): #895 dark gray, #803 lime, #897 mustard, #866 medium gray, #840 rust, #810 fuchsia, #806 blackberry, #879 dark green, and #896 violet, 1 skein each.

NEEDLES
Size 10 (6 mm). Adjust needle size if necessary to obtain the correct gauge.

NOTIONS
Tapestry needle; safety pins.

GAUGE
24 sts and 25 rows = 4" (10 cm) in k1, p1 rib, relaxed. Exact gauge is not critical for this project.

STRIP 3

With mustard, CO 6 sts. Work k1, p1 rib with edge stitches until piece measures 27" (68.5 cm) from beg. Change to medium gray and cont in patt until piece measures 57" (145 cm) from beg. Change to dark gray and cont in patt until piece measures 90" (229 cm) from beg. BO all sts.

STRIP 4

With rust, CO 8 sts. Work k1, p1 rib with edge stitches until piece measures 18" (45.5 cm) from beg. Change to blackberry and cont in patt until piece measures 54" (137 cm) from beg. Change to violet and cont in patt until piece measures 83" (211 cm) from beg. BO all sts.

FINISHING

Weave in loose ends. Gently block strips if needed. *Arrange strips*: Arrange the strips on the floor or large table in order from 1 to 4, with selvedges touching and aligning the CO edges. Shift the strips up or down to stagger them as foll: At the CO edge, make Strip 1 3" (7.5 cm) shorter than Strip 2; make Strip 3 2" (5 cm) shorter than Strip 2; make Strip 4 5" (12.5 cm) shorter than Strip 2. Smooth the strips along their length so they are lying flat and parallel with selvedges touching. Carefully pin the strips together temporarily using safety pins. *Place knots*: Measuring from the CO (medium gray) end of Strip 1, place knots (see Stitch Guide) between Strips 1 and 2 at the foll intervals: lime knot at 14" (35.5 cm), fuchsia knot at 21" (53.5 cm), lime knot at 25" (63.5 cm), fuchsia knot at 29" (73.5 cm), lime knot at 33" (84 cm), fuchsia knot at 42" (106.5 cm), fuchsia knot at 46" (117 cm), lime knot at 51" (129.5 cm), fuchsia knot at 56" (142 cm), fuchsia knot at 61" (155 cm), lime knot at 69" (175.5 cm), fuchsia knot at 74" (188 cm). Measuring from the CO (mustard) end of Strip 3, place knots between Strips 2 and 3 at the foll intervals: fuchsia knot at 14" (35.5 cm), lime knot at 22" (56 cm), lime knot at 29" (73.5 cm), fuchsia knot at 37" (94 cm), lime knot at 41" (104 cm), lime knot at 49" (124.5 cm), lime knot at 58" (147.5 cm), fuchsia knot at 66" (167.5 cm), lime knot at 70" (178 cm). Measuring from the CO (rust) end of Strip 4, place knots between Strips 3 and 4 at the foll intervals: fuchsia knot at 15" (38 cm), fuchsia knot at 22" (56 cm), lime knot at 28" (71 cm), fuchsia knot at 32" (81.5 cm), lime knot at 41" (104 cm), fuchsia knot at 45" (114.5 cm), fuchsia knot at 51" (129.5 cm), lime knot at 60" (152.5 cm), lime knot at 65" (165 cm), fuchsia knot at 70" (178 cm). Remove safety pins.

ROSEBUD SCARF
SASHA KAGAN

Sasha Kagan is well known for the use of floral motifs in her knitwear designs. The rose, with its connotations of love, has been a continuing theme in her work, and here the motifs she uses are reminiscent of Mid-European folk embroidery. She centered a large, detailed, single rose in the pointed ends of her scarf and surrounded it with delicate sprigs. The central portion of the scarf is textured in a subtle diagonal pattern for interest, and the scarf is finished with a crocheted edge. The warm rose colors on a tweedy black background and a deep, colorful fringe give her scarf a Spanish feel, like something a flamenco dancer might toss—with an artful flourish—about her neck.

NOTES
- ❖ Use separate balls or bobbins of yarn for each motif and carry the background yarn (MC) behind from selvedge to selvedge, securing the floats on every other stitch.
- ❖ See Glossary for crochet instructions.

SCARF

With MC, CO 3 sts. Purl 1 row on WS. Beg with Row 1, work in patt from Rosebud chart, inc 4 sts using the cable cast-on method (see Glossary) at beg of every row, as shown on chart—99 sts after Row 24 has been completed. Cont in patt from chart until Row 76 has been completed. Rep Rows 77–82 from chart for diagonal rib patt piece measures about 31" (79 cm) from beg point, ending with Row 82. Reverse the direction of the diagonal rib by rep Rows 83–88 until piece measures about 54½" (138.5 cm) from beg point, or 7½" (19 cm) less than desired length from point to point, ending with Row 88. Work Rows 89–164 from chart once, binding off 4 sts at beg of each row beginning with Row 141 as shown on chart—3 sts rem after Row 164 has been completed. BO rem sts.

FINISHED SIZE
14½" (37 cm) wide and 62" (157.5 cm) long from point to point, not including 4½" (11.5 cm) fringe at each end.

YARN
Rowan Yorkshire Tweed 4-Ply (100% wool; 120 yd [110 m]/25 g): #283 whiskers (black, MC), 8 balls; #274 brilliant (red), #273 glory (gold), #271 cheerful (teal), #266 highlander (green), #269 blessed (dusty rose), #275 foxy (burgundy tweed), 1 ball each. Rowan Wool Cotton (50% Merino wool, 50% cotton; 123 yd [112 m]/50 g): #943 flower (pink), #910 gypsy (wine), 1 ball each. Yarn distributed by Westminster Fibers.

NEEDLES
Size 4 (3.25 mm): straight. Adjust needle size if necessary to obtain the correct gauge.

NOTIONS
Crochet hook size B/1 (2.5-mm); tapestry needle.

GAUGE
27 sts and 33 rows = 4" (10 cm) in St st intarsia.

FINISHING

Weave in loose ends behind their corresponding motifs.

Edging:

Row 1: With crochet hook, MC, and RS facing, work a row of single crochet (sc) around entire edge of scarf, working 3 sc in each center point and corner.

Row 2: Change to burgundy tweed and work as for Row 1.

Row 3: Change to pink and work as for Row 1. Fasten off last st and weave in ends.

Fringe: Cut forty 10" (25.5-cm) strands each of *red, burgundy tweed, pink, dusty rose, gold. Fold each length in half and use crochet hook to attach 100 strands to each end of scarf, repeating the color order given at *. Trim ends even.

Block lightly.

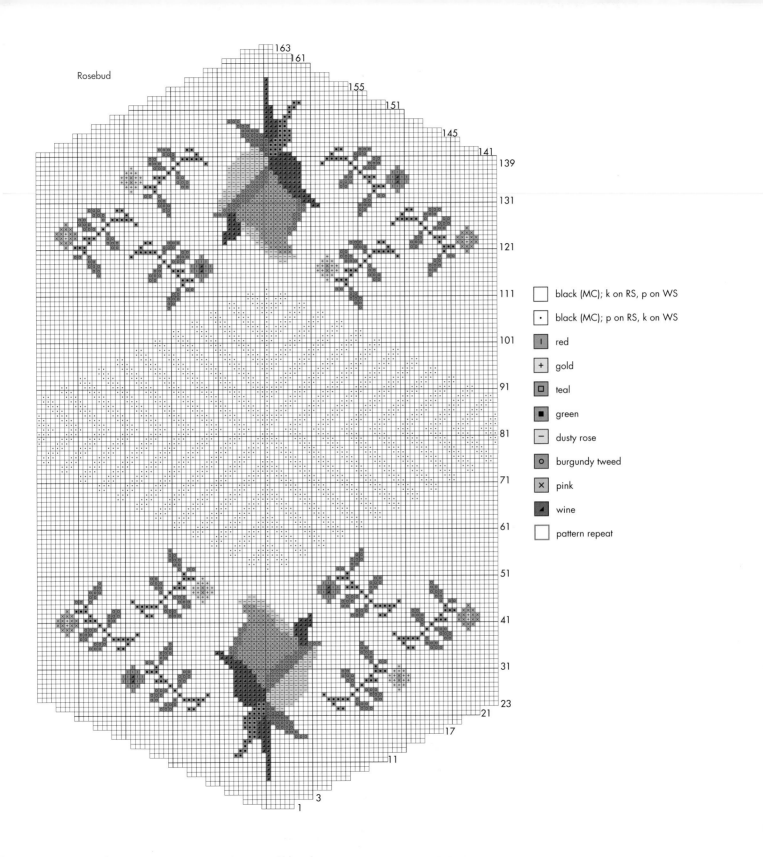

Rosebud

	black (MC); k on RS, p on WS
·	black (MC); p on RS, k on WS
I	red
+	gold
□	teal
■	green
−	dusty rose
o	burgundy tweed
×	pink
◢	wine
	pattern repeat

1 3 11 17 21 23 31 41 51 61 71 81 91 101 111 121 131 139 141 145 151 155 161 163

MISTY GARDEN
JO SHARP

Jo Sharp finds that working with a painted yarn always brings a surprise. "I never know how the fabric will look until it's finished. If I work on a straight stockinette-stitch piece, the result is stripey. However, when I work with a lacey stitch or crochet, the result is variegated and irregular." In this case, the soft, modulated colors of the yarn she's used have a painterly feel, like an antique watercolor of a misty rose garden. The yarn's colors and mood work well with the old-fashioned, graceful Feather and Fan stitch pattern.

SCARF

CO 38 sts. Work in patt as foll:

Row 1: (RS) Knit.
Row 2: Purl.
Row 3: K1, *[k2tog] 3 times, [yo, k1] 6 times, [k2tog] 3 times; rep from * to last st, k1.
Row 4: Knit.
Rep Rows 1–4 until piece measures about 59" (150 cm) from beg. BO all sts.

FINISHING

Weave in loose ends. Block lightly, if desired.

FINISHED SIZE
7" (18 cm) wide and 59" (150 cm) long, after blocking.

YARN
Jo Sharp Rare Comfort Kid Mohair Infusion (80% kid mohair, 15% polyamide, 5% wool; 95 yd [87 m]/25 g): #617 rosehip, 3 balls. Yarn distributed by www.josharp.com.au.

NEEDLES
Size 8 (5 mm). Adjust needle size if necessary to obtain the correct gauge.

NOTIONS
Tapestry needle.

GAUGE
21 sts and 20 rows = 4" (10 cm) in pattern st.

LADY ELEANOR ENTRELAC STOLE
KATHLEEN POWER JOHNSON

A good knitted design is a sound marriage of stitch pattern and yarn. In this case, Kathleen Power Johnson uses the faceted surface of entrelac to show off the beautiful nuances of handspun and hand-dyed yarn from La Lana Wools. Kathleen has named her stole Eleanor because its combination of rich, elegant colors and soft yet rustic hand suggest a garment that might have been worn by a medieval lady during a walk in the woods, maybe to keep a tryst or to dream by a castle fire. The long, knotted fringe adds a touch of drama and romance.

NOTES

❖ Gauge can be measured on an ordinary St st swatch at least 4" (10 cm) square. However, once you have completed several tiers, check the size of the finished rectangles in case you need to adjust needle size.

❖ Slip stitches as if to purl (pwise) with yarn in back, unless directed otherwise.

❖ You may find it helpful to use a stitch marker at the end of every section to keep them distinct, but remove the markers from the previous tier as you encounter them.

SCARF

BASE TRIANGLES
Using the backward-loop method (see Glossary), CO 56 sts.

FIRST TRIANGLE:
Row 1: (RS) K1, turn.
Row 2 and all WS rows: Purl all sts worked on last row.
Row 3: Sl 1, k1, turn.
Row 5: Sl 1, k2, turn.
Row 7: Sl 1, k3, turn.
Row 9: Sl 1, k4, turn.
Row 11: Sl 1, k5, turn.

FINISHED SIZE
23" (58.5 cm) wide and 70" (178 cm) long, after blocking, not including fringe.

YARN
La Lana Wools Forever Random Blends (60% wool, 40% mohair; 81 yd [74 m]/ 2 oz [57 g]): Faerie Queen, 15 skeins.

NEEDLES
Size 10½ (6.5 mm). Adjust needle size if necessary to obtain the correct gauge. You may also find it helpful to use a 32" (80-cm) or longer circular needle so the weight of the project can rest in your lap as it grows.

NOTIONS
Markers (m; optional); tapestry needle; size J/10 (6-mm) crochet hook for applying fringe; tapestry needle.

GAUGE
14 sts and 18 rows = 4" (10 cm) in St st. Each entrelac rectangle measures about 3½" (6.5 cm) wide *on the diagonal* (at right angles to the sides of the piece being worked).

Row 13: Sl 1, k6, turn.

Row 15: Sl 1, k7. Do not turn work.

Work six more triangles the same as the first—56 sts, 8 sts each in seven triangles. Turn work at end of seventh triangle.

TIER 1

Tier 1 is made up of a left side triangle, six full rectangles, and a right side triangle, as viewed from the RS of the work.

LEFT SIDE TRIANGLE

Row 1: (WS) K1, turn.

Row 2: K1f&b, turn.

Row 3: K1, p2tog, turn.

Row 4: K1, M1 (see Glossary), k1, turn.

Row 5: K1, p1, p2tog, turn.

Row 6 and all RS rows: Knit to last st, M1, k1.

Row 7: K1, p2, p2tog, turn.

Row 9: K1, p3, p2tog, turn.

Row 11: K1, p4, p2tog, turn.

Row 13: K1, p5, p2tog, turn.

Row 15: K1, p6, p2tog, do not turn—8 sts in left triangle.

Work the first rectangle of this tier as foll:

TIER 1 RECTANGLES

Row 1: (WS) With WS facing, pick up and purl 8 sts along selvedge of next triangle or rectangle as foll: *Insert tip of right needle under both legs of selvedge st from back to front, wrap yarn around needle pwise, and pull up a loop; rep from * until 8 sts have been picked up. Sl last st picked up to left needle and p2tog.

Row 2: K8, turn.

Row 3: Sl 1, p6, p2tog, turn.

Rows 4–15: Rep Rows 2 and 3 six more times. At the end of Row 15, do not turn.

Work the next rectangle same as the first. When a total of six rectangles for this tier have been completed, work a right side triangle as foll:

The wrong side of entrelac fabric shows a more rustic face: reverse stockinette stitch and exposed seams.

RIGHT SIDE TRIANGLE

Row 1: (WS) Pick up and purl 8 sts along selvedge of next triangle or rectangle, turn.

Row 2 and all RS Rows: Knit to end of sts in this section, turn.

Row 3: Sl 1, p5, k2tog, turn.

Row 5: Sl 1, p4, k2tog, turn.

Row 7: Sl 1, p3, k2tog, turn.

Row 9: Sl 1, p2, k2tog, turn.

Row 11: Sl 1, p1, k2tog, turn.

Row 13: Sl 1, k2tog, turn.

Row 15: K2tog. The rem single st will count as the first st picked up for the first rectangle in the next tier. Turn and transfer this st to the right needle.

TIER 2

Tier 2 is made up of seven full rectangles.

TIER 2 RECTANGLES

Row 1: (RS) With RS facing, pick up and knit 8 sts along selvedge of next triangle or rectangle. For the first rectangle in this tier *only*, the st rem from the previous triangle counts as the first picked up st. Sl last st picked up to left needle and ssk (see Glossary).

Row 2: P8, turn.

Row 3: Sl 1, k6, ssk, turn.

Rows 4–15: Rep Rows 2 and 3 six more times. At the end of Row 15, do not turn. Work a total of seven rectangles for this tier, ending with a RS row. Turn work, ready to work a WS row.

TIERS 3–35

Rep Tiers 1 and 2 sixteen more times, then work Tier 1 once more—56 sts.

FINAL TIER TRIANGLES

Row 1: (RS) With RS facing, pick up and knit 8 sts along selvedge of next triangle or rectangle. For the first triangle *only*, the st rem from the previous side triangle counts as the first picked up st. Sl last st picked up to left needle and ssk.

Row 2 and all WS Rows: Purl to end of sts in this section, turn.

Row 3: K2tog, k5, ssk, turn.

Use a circular needle, 32" or longer, when working a project as large as this shawl.

Row 5: K2tog, k4, ssk, turn.

Row 7: K2tog, k3, ssk, turn.

Row 9: K2tog, k2, ssk, turn.

Row 11: K2tog, k1, ssk, turn.

Row 13: K2tog, ssk, turn.

Row 15: Sl 1, ssk, psso, do not turn. The rem single st will count as the first st picked up for the next triangle.

Work a total of seven triangles. Fasten off last st.

FINISHING

Weave in loose ends. Block stole flat. With crochet hook and RS facing, loosely work a row of single crochet (see Glossary) across each short edge. **_Knotted fringe_**: Cut fifty-two 40" (101.5-cm) strands of yarn. With RS facing, attach 26 fringe strands evenly spaced to each short edge as foll: Fold each length in half forming a loop at the midpoint in the strand. With crochet hook, pull loop through one entire edge stitch, pass both cut ends through the loop, pull snug, and tie an overhand knot close to the finished edge. Work knotting as foll: *Working from right to left, skip the first strand of the first fringe, and tie one strand each from the first and second fringes tog with an overhand knot about 1" (2.5 cm) below the first row of knots. Cont across, tying one strand from each pair tog until you reach the left side; the last strand will not be knotted. Tie another row of knots about 1" (2.5 cm) below the previous row, this time tying the strands in their original pairs. Rep from * 2 more times—7 rows of knots total, including the initial knots at base of fringe. Trim ends even.

A deep knotted fringe at the ends of this scarf give it a dramatic flourish, but a series of thick tassels would be quite attractive, too.

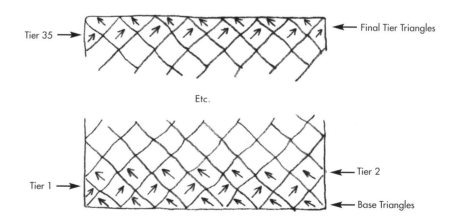

Irresistible color, imaginative piecework, and embellishment are the distinctive hallmarks of Kathryn Alexander's work. Her knitted garments fairly sing in their joyful exploration of the unexpected. For Kathryn, the process of knitting and inventing is as important as the outcome. She wants all her work to be so compelling that she can't lay it aside. "I pick the work up the first thing in the morning, think about it over lunch and dinner, and dream about it through the night." As she works, color and texture fly across her surfaces, keeping her hands and mind engaged. Each piece suggests another, and as she nears the completion of one, she anticipates beginning the next.

NOTES

✝ This yarn comes in a "knot," which is 10 strands, each 30" (76 cm) long for a total of 8.33 yd (7.6 cm).

✝ This yarn is made up of three individual 2-ply strands loosely twisted together. Separate each strand into its three parts and work with two of those parts held together, unless instructed otherwise.

✝ Circular needles are used to hold large numbers of live stitches to avoid having to transfer these stitches to and from a holder.

✝ Size 5 (3.75 mm) needles are used unless otherwise specified.

✝ Although colors #484, #592, #890, and #940 are not specifically mentioned in the row-by-row instructions, use them in the random stripes of the I-cord fringes and for other embellishments.

SCARF

SECTION 1
With #612 and size 5 (3.75 mm) needles, CO 10 sts. Work 33 rows St st. Cut yarn, leave sts on needle. (See illustration on page 60.)

SECTION 2
Change to #495. Work 33 rows rev St st. Cut yarn, leave sts on needle.

SECTION 3
Change to #503. Work 33 rows St st. BO all sts.

FINISHED SIZE
11" (28 cm) wide and 62" (157.5 cm) long, not including fringes and trims.

YARN
Paternayan Persian Yarn (100% wool; 8 yd [7.4 m]/⅕ oz [5.7 g]): #612, 6 knots; #503, #522, #662, and #853, 3 knots each; #301, #313, #332, #495, #513, #561, #573, #575, #582, #603, #630, #652, #693, #696, #700, #701, #723, #732, #751, #830, #862, #882, #890, #912, #931, and #952, 2 knots each; #342, #351, #484, #532, #541, #592, #633, #698, #699, #812, #832, #873, #893, #902, #922, and #940, 1 knot each. Yarn distributed by JCA.

NEEDLES
Size 5 (3.75 mm): three 32" (80-cm) circular (cir); one 8" (20-cm) double pointed (dpn). Size 1 (2.25 mm) and size 2 (2.75 mm): 2 dpn each. Size 7 (4.5 mm): any size for binding off. Adjust needle size if necessary to obtain the correct gauge.

NOTIONS
Stitch holders; tapestry needle; four ⅞" (2.2-cm) metal buttons for covering (Dritz brand used here); scrap of thin silk cloth, about 12" (30.5 cm) square.

GAUGE
17 sts and 23 rows = 4" (10 cm) in St st using two of the three 2-ply strands held together.

SECTION 4

Hold the strip with Sections 1, 2, and 3 horizontally, with the knit sides of Sections 1 and 3 facing you, and green Section 1 on the right. The side of the strip facing you now will be the RS of the work. Beg at the right-hand side and using #652, pick up and knit 51 sts along upper (selvedge) edge of strip. Work 5 rows St st, beg and ending with a WS row. Cut yarn, leave sts on needle.

SECTION 5

Change to #513. Knit 6 rows (3 garter ridges). Cut yarn, leave sts on needle.

SECTION 6

Change to #751. Work 6 rows St st, beg with a RS row. Cut yarn, leave sts on needle.

SECTION 7

Turn work upside down so the other long edge of the Section 1, 2, 3 strip is uppermost, with the knit sides of Sections 1 and 3 facing you, and blue Section 3 on the right. Beg at the right-hand side and using #912, pick up and knit 51 sts along edge of strip. Work 9 rows St st, beg and ending with a WS row. Cut yarn, leave sts on needle.

SECTION 8

Change to #952. Work 10 rows rev St st. Cut yarn, leave sts on needle.

SECTION 9

Change to #832. Work 10 rows rev St st. Cut yarn, leave sts on needle.

SECTION 10

Change to #701. Work 10 rows rev St st. Change to #873 and leaving a 45" (114-cm) tail to use later, work 4 rows St st. BO all sts loosely using larger needle. The #873 St st section will roll to the RS of the work. Piece should measure about 12" (30.5 cm) wide and 9½" (24 cm) high, with BO edge of Section 10 rolled.

SECTION 11 (FIRST FAIR ISLE SECTION)

Hold completed piece so that RS is facing you and the rolled edge of Section 10 runs vertically along the left side. With #882, pick up and knit 39 sts. Knit 1 row. On the next row (RS), change to size 2 (2.75-mm) needles. Separate the two strands of #882 and knit across with a single strand, working k1 into each of the two strands of every st on the needle—78 sts. (If you want to use up both attached strands of #882, alternate the two single strands every 2 rows until they are both used up, then join a new single strand of #882 if necessary.) Purl 1

A colorful I-cord fringe incorporates loose ends of yarn which would otherwise have to be woven in.

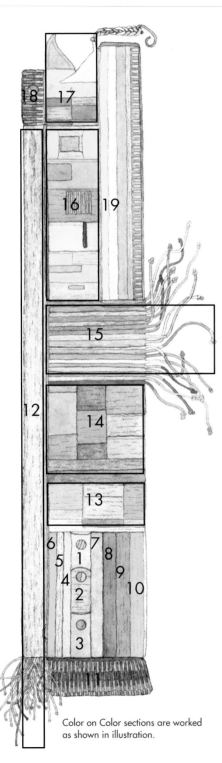

Color on Color sections are worked
as shown in illustration.

row with a single strand. Join a single strand of #662. Beg with a RS row, work 2x2 Fair Isle patt with a single strand of each color as foll: *RS rows:* *K2 with first color, k2 with second color; rep from * to last 2 sts, end k2 with first color; *WS rows:* *P2 with first color, p2 with second color; rep from * to last 2 sts, end p2 with first color. Use colors in the foll order (shown as first color/second color):

Rows 1–4: #882/#662.

Rows 5–6: #830/#662.

Rows 7–11: #830/ #630.

Rows 12–15: #853/#630.

Rows 16–18: #853/#696.

Row 19: #853/#612.

Rows 20–26: #931/#612. *At the same time*, on Row 25 *only*, purl all sts in color patt on RS to form a turning ridge.

Rows 27–28: #931/#652.

Rows 29–33: #862/#652.

Rows 34–35: #862/#522.

Row 36: #922/#522.

Rows 37–43: #922/#603.

Rows 44–46: #495/#603.

Rows 47–51: #700/#693. Do not cut yarns.

With smaller dpn and WS facing, place 1 loop from each st in garter row at the base of this section on a single dpn. Fold Fair Isle section in half along turning ridge at Row 25 with RS facing outward. Hold the needle with the picked-up loops in front, and the needle with the 78 live sts in back with WS facing. Using both colors from Row 51 held tog to make a double strand, use the three-needle method (see Glossary) to BO the beg and end of this section tog as foll: K3tog (the first loop on the front pick-up needle and the first two loops from the live sts on the back needle), *k3tog (the next loop of the front needle and the next two loops of the back needle), BO 1 st; rep from * until 2 sts rem on right needle. BO 1 st, cut yarn leaving a 45" (114-cm) tail, and draw tail through last st.

The Fair Isle section is still open along its two short sides. Close the side nearest to where you just finished as foll: Using two smaller dpn, place fourteen loops from along each side of the short opening on each needle. Holding the dpn tog, and working with both strands of the #700/#693 tail and larger needle, and using the three-needle method, BO sts tog to close this side. Fasten off last st. In the same manner, place fourteen loops from along each side of the other short opening on 2 dpn. Using both strands of the #873 tail and larger needle, work three-needle BO to close side. Fasten off last st.

SECTION 12 (STRIPED GARTER ST BAND)

With larger needle and two strands of #582, CO 211 sts, leaving a tail at least 12" (30.5 cm) long. With size 5 (3.75 mm) needles, knit 1 row. Cut yarn, leaving at least a 12" (30.5-cm) tail. Knit 2 rows each in the foll seven colors, using two strands of each color and leaving 12" (30.5-cm) tails at beg and end of each color: #561, #513, #503, #342, #332, #313, #522, and #603. Cut yarn, leaving a long tail as before, and leave sts on needle. There will be one size 5 (3.75 mm) cir needle holding the sts for this section, and one holding the sts at the end of Section 6.

I-cord fringe: Make striped I-cord fringes with single strands from the tails of each garter stripe. Scarf shown has 30 fringes and uses fewer than all the tails available. Using a single strand tail and a pair of size 2 (2.75 mm) dpn, pick up and knit 1 st from the edge of the garter stripe band, and CO 2 sts—3 sts. Work I-cord on 3 sts until there is about 3" (7.5 cm) of the color left, or until you feel like changing. To start a new color, fold a single strand of the new color in half about 3" (7.5 cm) from its end. Pull the folded loop of the new color through the base of the first st on the needle of the old color and place the loop on the needle. Work both the loop and the first st tog in the new color, then cont working with a single strand of the new color. Make striped I-cord fringes from 2" (5 cm) to 10" (25.5 cm) long, as desired, changing colors randomly. To finish each cord, cut yarn, draw tail through 3 sts on needle, and pull tightly to close. Weave each end into the center of the cord behind its own color, and tie a small overhand knot at the end of each cord.

SECTION 13

With rem cir needle, RS facing, and using two strands #873, pick up and knit 3 sts along rolled edge and 40 sts along the rem selvedge of the Sections 1–10 piece, and *at the same time* when you get to the edge of Section 1 (worked in green #612), let the edge of the section roll slightly to the front and pick up 2 sts in from the edge for a decorative effect—43 sts. Knit 2 rows, inc 2 sts on last row—45 sts. On the next row, (WS) set up positions of new colors as follows: K17 with #873, join two strands of #575 and k18, join two strands of #732 and k10.

Beg with a RS row, work intarsia garter st blocks with three colors in each row as foll: *RS rows:* K10 with first color, k18 with second color, k17 with third color; *WS rows:* K17 with third color, k18 with second color, k10 with first color. Cross the yarns at each color change to avoid leaving a hole, and rem consistent in how you cross to keep a neat appearance on both sides of the work. Use colors in the foll order (shown as first color/second color/third color):
Rows 1–6: #732/#575/#873.
Rows 7 and 8: #732/#575/#893.

Rows 9–14: #723/#522/#893.
Rows 15–26: #723/#522/#862.
Rows 27–34: #723/#503/#862. Cut all yarns.

SECTION 14

With #902, knit across the next row (RS), working k2tog at each color join—43 sts. Knit 7 more rows. Change to #351 and knit 8 rows, inc 2 sts in last row—45 sts.

Beg with a RS row, work intarsia garter st blocks with three colors in each row as foll: *RS rows:* K18 with first color, k13 with second color, k14 with third color; *WS rows:* K14 with third color, k13 with second color, k18 with first color. Cross the yarns at each color change as before as foll (shown as first color/second color/third color):
Rows 1–14: #301/#882/#662.
Rows 15–18: #301/#832/#662.
Rows 19–24: #332/#832/#662.
Beg with Row 25, work third color block in St st (knit last 14 sts of RS rows, purl first 14 sts of WS rows).
Rows 25–36: #332/#832/#612.
Beg with Row 37, work first color block in rev St st (purl first 18 sts on RS rows, knit last 18 sts on WS rows), cont to work second block in garter st, and third block in St st as established.
Rows 37–49: #582/#830/#612.
Rows 50–54: #582/#830/#532. Cut all yarns.

SECTION 15

This section is worked in 3-row stripes, leaving 12" (30.5-cm) tails at beg of RS rows for I-cord fringe as in Section 12. In order to have all the tails on the same side of the work, even though there are an odd number of rows, work each St st 3-row stripe as foll:
Row 1: (WS) Turn the work with WS facing. Using a tapestry needle, thread a single strand of yarn about 2 yd (2 m) long through the first st, and pull until the ends are even. Using both ends of this strand held tog, purl to end.
Row 2: (RS) Join a double strand of yarn, leaving a 12" (30.5-cm) tail at the beg of the row, knit to end.
Row 3: Turn work, purl to end, cut yarn leaving a 12" (30.5-cm) tail.
Work nine 3-row St st stripes in this manner with #699, #612, #351, #301, #931, #922, #882, #575, and #561.

Work the next nine 3-row stripes in rev St st as foll:
Row 1: (WS) Turn the work with WS facing. Using a tapestry needle, join a single strand of

Scarves don't have to be worked in a continuous fashion from one end to the next. Kathryn Alexander picked up stitches along the edges and worked at right angles to the body.

yarn through the first st as for Row 1 above, and using both ends of this strand held tog, knit to end.

Row 2: (RS) Join a double strand of yarn, leaving a 12" (30.5-cm) tail at the beg of the row, purl to end.

Row 3: Turn work, knit to end, cut yarn leaving a 12" (30.5-cm) tail.

Work nine 3-row rev St st stripes in this manner with #633, #723, #952, #853, #495, #693, #862, #662, and #573.

I-cord fringe: Make striped I-cord fringes as for Section 12, using double strands from the tails of the stripes, and changing colors randomly as before. Scarf shown has 19 fringes and uses fewer than all the tails available. Make striped I-cord fringes from 8" (20.5 cm) to 19" (48.5 cm) long, as desired, changing colors randomly. Finish fringe cords as in Section 12. Place first 19 sts at beg of RS row on holder—26 sts rem.

SECTION 16

Join #612 to rem sts with RS facing.

Rows 1–8: Work in St st, dec 1 st on first row—25 sts.

Row 9: K8 #612, join #812 and k7 (weaving #612 in behind every st), knit to end with #612.

Rows 10 and 11: Work St st in colors as established. Cut #812 after Row 11 has been completed.

Rows 12 and 13: Purl with #612 (1 garter ridge formed). Cut #612.

Rows 14–20: Join #723 and work in St st.

Row 21: K10 #723, join #698 and work to end.

Rows 22–24: Work St st intarsia with colors as established, crossing the yarns consistently at the color change to avoid leaving a hole and to keep a neat appearance on both sides of the work. Cut #698 after Row 24 has been completed.

Rows 25 and 26: Work in St st with #723.

Row 27: P15, k10.

Row 28: P10, k15.

Rows 29–36: Rep Rows 27–28 four times.

Row 37: Rep Row 27.

Row 38: K10, p15. Cut #723,

Rows 39–41: Join #503 and work in St st.

Row 42: P17 #503, join #541 and k2, p6 #503.

Rows 43–57: Work in St st with colors as established, weaving #503 in behind the 2-st column of #541.

Row 58: K17 #503, p2 #541, k6 #503. Cut both yarns.

Rows 59–62: Join #573 and work in rev St st.

Row 63: P4 #573, join #652 and work [k1 #652, k1 #573] 6 times, k1 #652, p8 #573.

Row 64: K8 #573, [p1 #652, k1 #573] 6 times, p1 #652, k4 #573.

Rows 65–76: Rep Rows 63–64 six times. Cut #652.

Rows 77 and 78: Knit with #573 (1 garter ridge formed). Cut #573.

Rows 79–84: Join #832 and work in St st.

Row 85: K14 #832, join #952 and k11.

Rows 86–96: Work in St st intarsia in colors as established. Cut #952 after Row 96 has been completed.

Rows 97 and 98: Work in St st with #832.

Row 99: Purl (1 garter ridge formed). Cut #832.

Row 100: Join #701 and purl across.

Row 101: K7, p13, k5.

Row 102: P5, k13, p7.

Rows 103 and 104: Rep Rows 101 and 102.

Row 105: K7, p2, join #952 and k9, join another double strand of #701 and p2, k5.

Row 106: P5 #701, k2 #701, p9 #952 crossing yarns at color joins on both ends of this block, k2 #701, p7 #701.

Rows 107–114: Rep Rows 105 and 106 four times.

Row 115: Rep Row 105. Cut #952.

Row 116: Rep Row 102.

Rows 117 and 118: Rep Rows 101 and 102.

Row 119: Knit across. Cut #701.

Rows 120–123: Join #633 and purl 4 rows. Cut #633. Place sts on a holder.

Attach garter st band: Using cir needle holding 51 live sts from Section 6 with WS facing, place 92 loops from selvedge edge of Sections 13, 14, and 15 on needle as foll: 20 sts from Section 13, 37 sts from Section 14, and 35 sts from Section 15—143 sts; 92 picked up loops, 51 live sts from Section 6. Hold this piece and Section 12 (striped garter st band) tog with WS touching and RS facing outwards. Join double strand of #751 to end with live sts from Section 6 and work three-needle BO to join 143 sts of garter st band to rest of piece. Cut #751 and fasten off. There will be 68 sts of garter st band rem on needle. Join #696 to rem garter band sts with RS facing and knit 2 rows.

Position main piece with garter band uppermost, RS facing, and the end of Section 16 on your right. Join a double strand of #862 to the upper selvedge of Section 16, and pick up and knit 68 sts from end of Section 16 to where garter st band joins the rest of the piece. With #862, [knit 1 row, purl 1 row] 2 times. Cut #862 leaving a tail about 1½ times as long as the 68-st section. Run this tail through all sts. Stretch the work to make sure the strand is not too tight, and the piece has the same flexibility as the rest of the knitting, and fasten off. The live sts threaded on the strand form a decorative edge.

With WS facing, place 68 loops from selvedge edge of Section 16 on needle. Fold garter band and main piece with RS touching and WS facing out. With needle holding picked-up loops from Section 16 in front, and needle holding garter band sts in back, join #751 at the side where the last join left off, and work three-needle BO to join rem garter band sts to main piece. Fasten off, leaving a 2-yd (2-m) tail of #751.

SECTION 17

Return 25 held sts at top of Section 16 to needle and join double strand of #696 with WS facing. Purl 1 row.

Row 1: (RS) Join #931 and k13, rejoin #696 and p12 *without* crossing the yarns at the color change to create a slit between the color blocks here that will form a buttonhole.

Row 2: K12 #696, p13 #931, again without crossing yarn at the color change.

Rows 3 and 4: Rep Rows 1 and 2. Cut yarns.

Row 5: Exchange color positions. Join #696 and k13, join #931 and p12, now crossing the yarns at the color change.

Row 6: K12 #931, p13 #696.

Rows 7–18: Rep Rows 5 and 6 six times. Cut yarns after Row 18 has been completed.

Row 19: Exchange color positions again. Join #931 and p13, join #696 and k12, crossing yarns at the color change.

Row 20: K12 #696 (garter ridge formed), k13 #931.

Row 21: P13 #931, k12 #696.

Row 22: P12 #696, k13 #931.

Rows 23 and 24: Rep Rows 21 and 22.

Row 25: Rep Row 21. Cut both yarns.

Rows 26–29: Join #495 and work 4 rows St st.

Row 30: P12, join second double strand of #495, purl to end.

Rows 31–33: Work in St st, working each section separately, without crossing yarns, to leave a buttonhole slit at center as before.

Rows 34–36: Work across all sts in St st with one doubled strand of yarn (no slit).

Row 37: Join #561 and k17, rejoin #495 and k8.

Row 38: P9 #495, p16 #561, crossing yarns at color change throughout.

The complexity of this scarf comes from an imaginative arrangement of simple knitted shapes worked in a myriad of clear, crayon colors.

Row 39: K15 #561, k10 #495.
Row 40: P11 #495, p14 #561.
Row 41: K13 #561, k12 #495.
Row 42: P13 #495, p12 #561.
Row 43: K11 #561, k14 #495.
Row 44: P15 #495, p10 #561. Place 15 sts in color #495 on holder and cut #495.
Row 45: Work continues on #561 sts only. K8, sl 1, k1, psso. Turn.
Even-numbered Rows 46–58: Purl.
Row 47: K7, sl 1, k1, psso—8 sts.
Row 49: K6, sl 1, k1, psso—7 sts.
Row 51: K5, sl 1, k1, psso—6 sts.
Row 53: K4, sl 1, k1, psso—5 sts.
Row 55: K3, sl 1, k1, psso—4 sts.
Row 57: K2, sl 1, k1, psso—3 sts.
Transfer rem 3 sts of #561 triangle to size 5 dpn (3.75 mm). Work striped I-cord for 32" (81.5 cm), changing colors randomly. Fasten off and weave in ends as for I-cord fringes in Section 12. Chain cord as if working a crochet chain to create a braided effect.

With RS facing, return 15 held sts to needle and join doubled strand of #575.
Row 1: (RS) Sl 1, k1, psso, k11, p1, k1—14 sts.
Row 2: K1, p13.
Row 3: Sl 1, k1, psso, k10, p1, k1—13 sts.
Row 4: K1, p12.
Row 5: Sl 1, k1, psso, k9, p1, k1—12 sts.
Row 6: K1, p11.
Row 7: Sl 1, k1, psso, k8, p1, k1—11 sts.
Row 8: K1, p10.
Row 9: Sl 1, k1, psso, k7, p1, k1—10 sts.
Row 10: K1, p9.
Row 11: Sl 1, k1, psso, k6, p1, k1—9 sts.
Row 12: K1, p8.
Row 13: Sl 1, k1, psso, k5, p1, k1—8 sts.
Row 14: K1, p7.
Row 15: Sl 1, k1, psso, k4, p1, k1—7 sts.
Row 16: K1, p6.
Row 17: Sl 1, k1, psso, k3, p1, k1—6 sts.
Row 18: K1, p5.
Row 19: Sl 1, k1, psso, k2, p1, k1—5 sts.

Use leftover yarns and simple embroidery to further embellish this scarf.

Row 20: K1, p4.

Row 21: Sl 1, k1, psso, k1, p1, k1—4 sts.

Row 22: K1, p3.

Row 23: Sl 1, k1, psso, p1, k1—3 sts.

Row 24: Knit.

Row 25: K3tog. Fasten off.

SECTION 18 (SECOND FAIR ISLE SECTION)

Hold completed piece so that the WS is facing you, with the striped garter band running along the top when viewed. Using the long tail of #751 left over from attaching the garter band, pick up and knit 23 sts along selvedge of Section 17. Cut #751 and join a single strand of #652. Change to size 2 (2.75-mm) needles, and knit across with the single strand, working k1 into each of the two strands of every st on the needle—46 sts. Purl 1 row with a single strand of #652. Join a single strand of #884. Beg with a RS row, work 2x2 Fair Isle patt with a single strand of each color as foll: *RS rows:* *K2 with first color, k2 with second color; rep from * to last 2 sts, k2 with first color; *WS rows:* *P2 with first color, p2 with second color; rep from * to last 2 sts, p2 with first color. Use colors in the foll order (shown as first color/second color):

Rows 1–4: #652/#884.

Rows 5–7: #662/#884.

Rows 8–10: #662/#952.

Rows 11–13: #699/#952.

Rows 14–20: #699/#351. At the same time, *on Row 16 only,* knit all sts in color patt on WS to form a turning ridge.

Rows 21–23: #662/#351.

Rows 24 and 25: #662/#890.

Rows 26–30: #603/#890. Do not cut yarns.

With smaller dpn and WS facing, place 1 loop from each st in the garter row at the base of this section on a single dpn. Fold Fair Isle section in half along turning ridge at Row 16 with RS facing outward. Hold the needle with the picked-up loops in front, and the needle with the 23 live sts in back with WS facing. Using both colors from Row 30 held tog to make a double strand, work three-needle BO with larger needle to join the beg and end of this section together as foll: K3tog (the first loop on the front pick-up needle and the first two loops from the live sts on the back needle), *k3tog (the next loop of the front needle and the next two loops of the back needle), BO 1 st; rep from * until 2 sts rem on right needle. BO 1 st, cut yarn leaving a 20" (51-cm) tail, and draw tail through last st. Use yarn tails to invisibly seam open side at end of scarf closed. Sew other side to edge of garter st band. Weave in any rem ends.

SECTION 19

With double strands of #732 and #662, size 5 (3.75 mm) needles, and using the knitted method (see Glossary), CO 110 sts, alternating colors (*CO 1 with #732, CO 1 with #662; rep from *). On the next row (WS), purl across working 1 st in each color alternately (p1 #732, p1 #662; rep from *). Cut #662.

Rows 1–3: Knit with #732 (garter ridge formed).

Rows 4 and 5: Work in St st. Cut #732 after Row 5 has been completed.

Rows 6–11: Join #522 and work in St st. Cut #522 after Row 11 has been completed.

Rows 12–18: Join #612 and work in St st. Cut #612 after Row 18 has been completed.

Rows 19–22: Join #693 and knit 4 rows (2 garter ridges formed). Cut #693 after Row 22 has been completed.

Row 23: Join #575 and knit across. Do not cut yarn. Join #700.

Row 24: *P1 #575, p1 #700; rep from * to end.

Row 25: *K1 #700, p1 #575; rep from * to end.

Row 26: *K1 #575, p1 #700; rep from * to end.

Row 27: Rep Row 25. Cut #575.

Row 28: Knit across with #700. Cut #700.

Change to double strand of #830, and BO using larger needle— st rem. Do not cut yarn. With RS facing, and size 5 (3.75-mm) needles, cont around the corner and pick up and knit 17 sts along short side of Section 19—18 sts. Knit 1 row on WS (garter ridge formed). Join double strand of #575, and work *k1 #575, k1 #830; rep from * to end. Cut #575. BO all sts on next row as if to knit with #830. Weave in ends.

With size 5 (3.75-mm) needles and WS facing, place 110 sts from rem selvedge of Sections 16 and 17 on one needle. With another size 5 (3.75-mm) needle and WS facing, pick up 110 loops from the top of the first row of #732 and #662 sts of Section 19; do not pick up loops from the two-color CO. Hold pieces tog with RS touching and WS facing outwards. Join double strand of #931 to one end, and using larger needle, work three-needle BO to join pieces. Cut #931 and fasten off.

Return 19 held sts of Section 15 to size 5 (3.75-mm) needle with RS facing. Join double strand #662 and knit 1 row. Using a separate needle and the same yarn, with RS facing, pick up and knit 19 sts along rem selvedge of Section 19. Hold pieces tog with WS touching and RS facing outwards. Work three-needle BO to join pieces. Cut yarn and fasten off.

FINISHING

Weave in any remaining ends.

Buttons: Make four button covers in random stripes as foll: With a single strand and size 1 (2.25-cm) needles, CO 14 sts. Work 15 rows St st changing colors as desired. BO all sts. Cut four small squares of silk cloth the same size as the button covers. For each button, place square of silk on the button, then the knitted cover (knit side out), and attach to button according to directions on the button package. Attach one button each in Sections 1, 2, and 3, centered from side to side, and about 1" (2.5 cm) down from the top of each section as shown. Attach rem button to the RS of Section 18, centered vertically on the section, and about 2" (5 cm) from the end of the scarf. *Attach buttons:* Hold 1-yd (1-m) single strands each of two randomly chosen colors tog and fold in half. Poke the loop of the fold through the shank of the button, then pass all four cut ends through the loop and pull snug to anchor the strands to the button. Position the buttons as given above, and use a tapestry needle to bring each pair of strands to the back of the scarf, one color on each side of a stitch. Tie all four ends in an overhand knot close to the scarf. With size 5 (3.75 mm) needles and working the double strand of each color separately, pick up and knit 3 sts from back of scarf and work a 3" (7.5-cm) I-cord with each color. Fasten off and weave in ends. Tie the two cords tog in a decorative knot.

Button loops: Make one button loop as given below, using #301 on the RS of scarf, on the join bet Section 6 and the garter band, about 2" (5 cm) from the end of the scarf. Make the other button loop using #698 on the WS of scarf, on the join bet Section 16 and the garter band, about 10" (25.5 cm) from the end of Section 18 (second Fair Isle section). To make button loop, cut a single strand about 24" (60 cm) long and fold it in half. Poke the folded loop through the eye of a tapestry needle, and pass it through the BO ridge at the desired location. Pull the loop out for a few inches and remove the needle. Pass the cut ends through the loop and pull snug to anchor it. Using a single strand and size 2 (2.75-cm) needles, pick up and knit 1 st from BO ridge, then CO 2 sts using the knitted method. Work I-cord for about 10 rows, or until loop is long enough to accommodate one of your buttons. Fasten off, and use tail to secure the other end of the button loop to the ridge.

I-cord doodad: Using a double strand and size 5 (3.75 mm) needles, make a 3-st randomly striped I-cord about 8" (20.5 cm) long. Fasten off. Tack one end to scarf, then coil the I-cord out from the center in a spiral, tacking it to the scarf as you go. Weave in ends. Make as many doodads as you like. For this scarf, there is one doodad on the WS, on the corner where Sections 6, 13, and garter band Section 12 all meet.

TURKISH TREASURE
MARI LYNN PATRICK

For the motifs in this fluid crocheted scarf, Mari Lynn Patrick drew from ancient patterns found in traditional knitted socks from the Near East. She used jewel colors—some dark and some light—for a combination as rich and vibrant as those in an antique Turkish carpet. To save having to weave in the many ends of yarn, she worked the scarf lengthwise, leaving long tails of yarn at the beginning and end of each row to form a ready-made fringe.

NOTES

❖ This scarf is designed with a self fringe. At the beginning and end of each row there are 10" (25.5-cm) lengths of each color used in the row left free to form the fringe.

❖ The yarns are cut at the end of every row and restarted at the beginning; all rows are worked from the right side.

❖ Colors not in use are carried across the top of the previous row and enclosed by the single crochet stitches of the current row.

❖ See Glossary for crochet instructions.

SCARF

With dark green, ch 266, leaving 10" (25.5 cm) free at beg of chain.

Row 1: (RS, Row 1 of Turkish chart) Work 1 sc in 2nd ch from hook and in each ch to end—265 sc. Cut yarn, leaving a 10" (25.5-cm) tail, and finish off last st by pulling tail through the loop just worked.

Row 2: (RS, Row 2 of Turkish chart) Return to beg of row and join dark green and light green, leaving 10" (25.5-cm) tails of each color free at beg of row. Work 265 sc according to chart (11 reps of patt, plus 1 end st), enclosing the color not in use by laying it on top of the previous row and crocheting around it.

Cut both yarns, leaving 10" (25.5-cm) tails, and finish off last st. Cont through Row 27 of chart, working in sc with the RS always facing, and leaving 10" (25.5-cm) tails of yarns used.

FINISHED SIZE
6½" (16.5 cm) wide and 66" (167.5 cm) long, not including fringe.

YARN
Berroco Softwist (41% wool, 59% rayon; 100 yd [92 m]/50 g): #9426 viridian (dark green), #9428 mushroom (beige), and #9440 cilantro (lime green), 2 skeins each; #9438 Tupelo honey (gold), #9468 blue moon (light blue), #9478 alizarin (burgundy), #9467 amethyst (pink), and #9439 ginger (dark orange), 1 skein each.

HOOK
Size I/9 (5.5-mm) crochet hook. Adjust hook size if necessary to obtain the correct gauge.

NOTIONS
Tapestry needle.

GAUGE
16 sts and 18 rows = 4" (10 cm) in single crochet colorwork patt from chart.

FINISHING

Join dark green at one short end of scarf with RS facing. Letting the fringe tails fall to the back of the scarf, work 26 sc along short edge, work (sc, ch 1, sc) all in corner st. Cut yarn, leaving a 10" (25.5-cm) tail for fringe, and fasten off last st. Join yarn to other short end with RS facing, and work the same as the first end, but do not cut yarn. *Edging*: Ch 1, *working reverse single crochet (from left to right, also called crab stitch), work 1 sc in next sc, ch 1, skip 1 sc; rep from * to corner, work (sc, ch 1, sc) all in corner st; rep from * until you have worked around all four sides. Cut yarn and fasten off last st. Pin scarf to measurements and block, squaring short ends as necessary. Trim fringe evenly.

Turkish

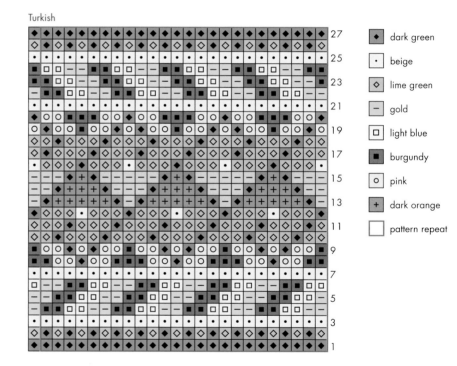

- ◆ dark green
- · beige
- ◇ lime green
- − gold
- □ light blue
- ■ burgundy
- ○ pink
- + dark orange
- ☐ pattern repeat

"Shippo" is the Japanese word for "tail," a fitting name for this small, triangular scarf that has more tail than triangle. What makes the scarf an especially charming accessory is the graphic placement of colors and the crinkly surface, a texture that results from its unusual yarns—a strand of linen paper and a strand of silk-embedded stainless steel held together. The scarf wraps around the neck, and the tails can be tied or left to fall on the neck or shoulder. The scarf's simple design and use of nontraditional fibers are characteristic of the unusual knitwear created by the design team of Setsuko Torii and Masami Fukui.

NOTE

❖ Scarf is not symmetrical. After washing and blocking, the point will be about 22" (56 cm) from one end, and 30" (76 cm) from the other end.

BASIC SCARF

With a strand of paper and a strand of silk stainless held tog, CO 3 sts. *Inc section*: Beg with a RS row, work St st for 6 rows, inc 1 st at end of last row—4 sts. Rep the last 6 rows three more times—7 sts; 24 rows completed. Work 4 rows St st, inc 1 st at end of last row—8 sts. Rep the last 4 rows nine more times—17 sts; 64 rows completed. Work 2 rows St st, inc 1 st at end of last row—18 sts. Work 4 rows St st, inc 1 st at end of last row—19 sts. Rep the last 6 rows three more times—25 sts; 88 rows completed. Work 2 rows St st, inc 1 st at end of last row—26 sts. Rep the last 2 rows sixteen more times—42 sts; 122 rows completed; piece should measure about 24½" (62 cm) from beg. *Dec section*: Work 2 rows St st, dec 1 st at end of last row—41 sts rem. Rep the last 2 rows fifteen more times—26 sts rem; 154 rows completed. Work 4 rows St st, dec 1 st at end of last row—25 sts rem. Rep the last 4 rows eleven more times—14 sts rem; 202 rows completed. Work St st for 6 rows, dec 1 st at end of last row—13 sts rem. Rep the last 6 rows four more times—9 sts rem; 232 rows completed. Work St st for 8 rows, dec 1 st at end of last row—8 sts rem. Rep the last 8 rows five more times—3 sts rem; 280 rows completed; piece should measure about 56" (142 cm) from beg. BO all sts.

FINISHED SIZE

52" (132 cm) long and 9¼" (23.5 cm) at widest point, after washing and blocking.

YARN

Habu Textiles A-60 Shosenshi Paper (100% linen paper with viscose sizing; 840 yd [755 m]/3 oz [85 g] skein). Habu Textiles A-20 and A-21, 1/20 Silk Stainless (69% silk, 31% stainless steel; 615 yd [550 m]/1 oz [28 g] cone). For striped scarf: A-60 Shosenshi Paper #113 brick, #115 gray-beige, and #116 wine, 1 skein each; A-20 Silk Stainless #02 black, A-21 #04 top brown, 1 cone each. For olive and black scarf: A-60 Shosenshi Paper #114 yellow-green (olive) and #119 sumi (black), 1 skein each; A-21 Silk Stainless #04 top brown and A-20 Silk Stainless #02 black, 1 cone each.

NEEDLES

Size 7 (4.5 mm). Adjust needle size if necessary to obtain the correct gauge.

NOTIONS

Tapestry needle.

GAUGE

16½ sts and 20 rows = 4" (10 cm) in St st with both strands held together, before washing; 18 sts and 22 rows = 4" (10 cm) in St st after washing and blocking.

FINISHING

Weave in loose ends. Roll scarf into a ball and knead gently by hand in cold or lukewarm water. Spread out to dry—the texture will be more interesting if you do not flatten, stretch, or iron the piece.

OLIVE AND BLACK SCARF (not shown)

Work as for basic scarf changing colors as foll. With olive paper and top brown silk stainless, CO and work St st until piece measures 6½" (16.5 cm) from beg. *Change to black silk stainless and work for 4" (10 cm), then change to top brown silk stainless and work for 5" (12.5 cm); rep from * once more; piece should measure 24½" (62 cm) from beg, and inc section should be completed. Change to black paper and black silk stainless and work for 3½" (9 cm). **Change to top brown silk stainless and work for 4" (10 cm), then change to black silk stainless and work for 4" (10 cm); rep from ** once more—piece should measure 44" (112 cm) from beg. Change to top brown silk stainless and work to end.

STRIPED SCARF

Work as for basic scarf using colors as foll. With brick paper and top brown silk stainless, CO and work St st until piece measures 5½" (14 cm) from beg. Change to gray-beige paper and work for 10½" (26.5 cm). Change to wine paper and work for 8½" (21.5 cm); piece should measure 24½" (62 cm) from beg, and inc section should be completed. Change to gray-beige paper and black silk stainless and work for 4 rows, ending with a WS row. Using black silk stainless throughout, work stripes in the foll paper colors: [2 rows wine, 2 rows gray-beige] 3 times, [2 rows brick, 2 rows gray-beige] 3 times, [2 rows wine, 2 rows gray-beige] 3 times—piece should measure 32½" (82.5 cm) from CO edge and 8" (20.5 cm) from beg of decs. Work with gray-beige paper and black silk stainless to end.

VINTAGE VELVET
LISA DANIELS

Elegant and long, soft as silk, this plush scarf wraps twice around the neck with ends to spare. Look closely and you'll see that the cable pattern is the same on both sides. Lisa Daniels has made the pattern reversible by using a ribbed pattern for the cable panel and by turning the cable on alternate sides of the scarf. A wash in hot water and a spin in the dryer give the chenille fabric the shimmer and feel of vintage velvet. Wear the scarf with a silky lingerie top or a tailored jacket.

> **NOTE**
> ❖ The cable crossings alternate between the two sides of the scarf.

SCARF

CO 34 sts. Work in patt as foll:

Row 1: K1, [p2, k2] 2 times, p2, place marker (pm), [k1, p1] 6 times, pm, [p2, k2] 2 times, p2, k1.

Row 2: K1, p1, [k2, p2] 2 times, k1, slip marker (sl m), [k1, p1] 6 times, sl m, k1, [p2, k2] 2 times, p1, k1.

Rows 3 and 4: Rep Rows 1 and 2.

Row 5: K1, [p2, k2] 2 times, p2, sl 6 sts onto cn and hold in back, [k1, p1] 3 times, work 6 sts from cn as [k1, p1] 3 times, [p2, k2] 2 times, p2, k1.

Row 6: Rep Row 2.

Rows 7–14: Rep Rows 1 and 2 four times.

Row 15: Rep Row 1.

Row 16: K1, p1, [k2, p2] 2 times, k1, sl 6 sts onto cn and hold in back, [k1, p1] 3 times, work 6 sts from cn as [k1, p1] 3 times, k1, [p2, k2] 2 times, p1, k1.

Rows 17–22: Rep Rows 1 and 2 three times.

Rep Rows 1–22 until almost all the yarn has been used, ending with Row 9 or Row 20 (4 rows past the last cable crossing row), and leaving a tail at least 4 times the width of the scarf for binding off. BO all sts in patt.

FINISHED SIZE
5" (13.5 cm) wide 68" (172.5 cm) long, after washing and felting.

YARN
Muench Yarns Touch Me (72% rayon microfiber, 28% wool; 61 yd [56 m]/ 50 g): #3618 toast, 5 skeins.

NEEDLES
Size 8 (5 mm). Adjust needle size if necessary to obtain the correct gauge.

NOTIONS
Cable needle (cn); markers (m); tapestry needle.

GAUGE
26 sts and 22 rows = 4" (10 cm) in reversible cable patt before washing and felting; scarf measures about 5¼" (13.5 cm) wide and 68" (173 cm) long before finishing.

FINISHING

Weave in loose ends. ***Felting:*** Touch Me projects lose about 10% of their original size in the final process. I recommend the following general guidelines. Place scarf in a lingerie bag, or other washing bag, then place in the washing machine with some old T-shirts or an old sheet. To felt a larger piece (bigger than the scarf shown here), place it directly in the washing machine with similar items without the washing bag. The goal is to have a large enough load that the machine will balance properly while avoiding clothes that could transfer color or lint to your finished item. Set the machine for a hot wash (yes, that's right—hot), add a small amount of mild detergent, and run through a full cycle. Place scarf in the dryer and dry until it is still damp to the touch. Lay flat and pat into shape to finish drying.

The antiqued finish on this scarf is the result of a wash in hot water and a quick spin in the dryer.

Annie Modesitt is an imaginative knitter who claims that she was afraid to try lace patterns until she learned how to chart them. Once she understood how to work lace from a charted pattern, a whole new world of possibilities unfolded, allowing her to explore the various ways that yarnovers and decreases work together to create a lace fabric. In her original idea for this scarf, she had placed the lacey leaf motifs in the center. As she worked on her swatch, she began moving the leaves out to the sides until they became the outer edge of the scarf and turned her original design concept inside out. She added a border of slip-stitch double knit to keep the scarf edges from rolling and to provide a bit of definition to the leaves. Although simple, this edging technique takes a few minutes to master. Annie suggests trying it for a few rows on a practice swatch before you start the scarf.

STITCH GUIDE

Ssk: Slip 2 sts individually kwise (knitwise), return these 2 sts to the left needle, and k2tog through the back loops.

Sssk: Slip 3 sts individually kwise, return these 3 sts to left needle, k3tog through the back loops.

Ssp: Slip 2 sts individually kwise, return these 2 sts to left needle, and p2tog through the back loops.

NOTES

❖ Scarf is worked in two identical sections, beginning at the center back neck. The cast-on edges are seamed together during the finishing process.

❖ The stitch count for the charted pattern changes from row to row.

FINISHED SIZE
About 5" (12.5 cm) wide and 78" (198 cm) long from tip to tip, after blocking.

YARN
Karabella Aurora 8 (100% Merino; 98 yd [90 m]/50 g): #11 light olive, 4 balls.

NEEDLES
Size 7 (4.5 mm). Adjust needle size if necessary to obtain the correct gauge.

NOTIONS
Markers (m); tapestry needle.

GAUGE
18 sts and 26 rows = 4" (10 cm) in St st.

SCARF HALF

(Make two) Using the long-tail method (see Glossary), CO 10 sts. Beg with set-up row, work through Row 8 of Leaf chart (you may find it helpful to place a marker where indicated by the line on chart)—32 sts. Work Rows 9–28 eleven times, or until scarf is just less than half the desired total length, ending with Row 28—32 sts. Work Rows 29–40. *Next row*: (Row 41 of chart) Work until there are 12 sts on right needle counting yarnovers and removing the marker (you should have just worked the second k2tog of the row), join a second ball of yarn and work to end. Work each leaf section separately through Row 51 of chart. For the leaf section that has only 1 st, cut yarn and draw tail through last st. Cont in patt on rem sts until Row 63 has been completed—1 st rem. Cut yarn and draw tail through last st.

FINISHING

Steam block pieces to finished measurements. With yarn threaded on a tapestry needle, sew CO edges of the two halves tog, aligning the "stems" at the base of each leaf. Weave in loose ends.

An ingenious slip-stitch edging makes a smooth finish along the waving sides of this scarf.

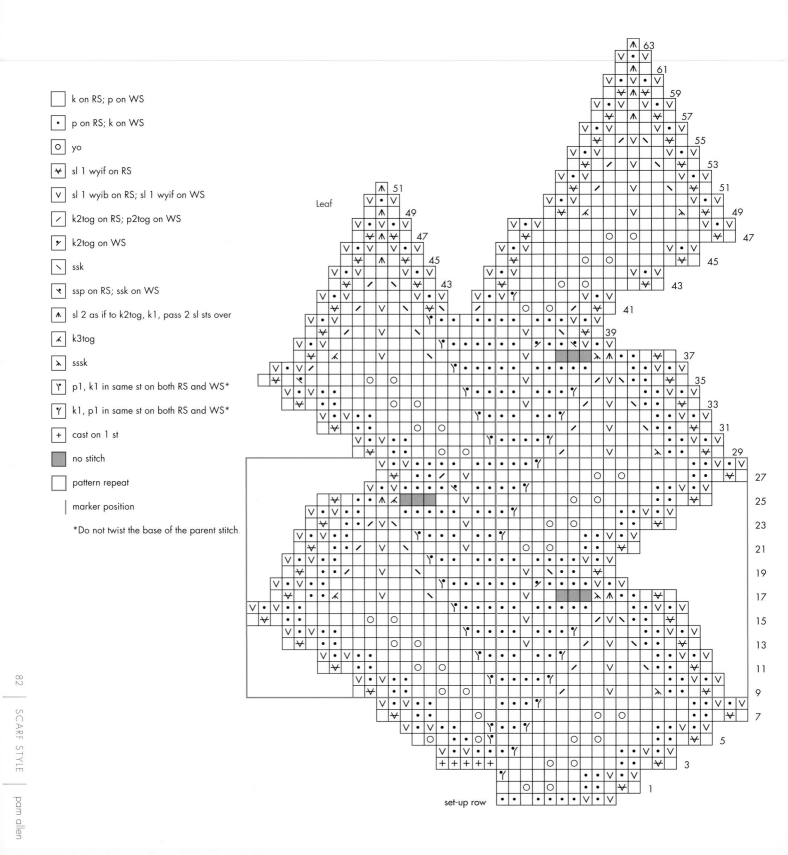

Leaf

k on RS; p on WS

• p on RS; k on WS

o yo

sl 1 wyif on RS

V sl 1 wyib on RS; sl 1 wyif on WS

/ k2tog on RS; p2tog on WS

k2tog on WS

\ ssk

ssp on RS; ssk on WS

sl 2 as if to k2tog, k1, pass 2 sl sts over

k3tog

sssk

p1, k1 in same st on both RS and WS*

k1, p1 in same st on both RS and WS*

+ cast on 1 st

no stitch

pattern repeat

marker position

*Do not twist the base of the parent stitch.

set-up row

TURTLENECK SHRUG
TEVA DURHAM

"The more I knit, the more I realize the joys and benefits of circular knitting," comments Teva Durham. "It's more efficient because there are fewer seams to sew. And it's easier to work complex stitch patterns because the right side of the fabric is always facing you."

In order to find more ways to work in the round, Teva gave herself a challenge when she designed this garment: What are the creative scarf possibilities in a simple tube? Her neck-warmer/shrug-cum-scarf is composed of three tubes—one for the neck and two for the arms. You can wear it as a bodyless turtleneck sweater with your arms through one or both sleeves, or you can wrap the sleeves around your neck like an everyday scarf. Worked in a simple rib pattern, the sleeves and neck expand but won't sag. And the soft yarn, a blend of lambswool and mohair, is light and comfortable to wear.

STITCH GUIDE

K3, P3 Rib: (multiple of 6 sts)
All Rnds: *K3, p3; rep from * to end.

SLEEVES

CO 66 sts. Place marker (pm) and join for working in the rnd, being careful not to twist sts. Work k3, p3 rib until piece measures about 23" (58.5 cm) from beg. *Next rnd:* BO 15 sts at beg of rnd, work in patt to end—51 sts rem. Work back and forth in rows as foll:
Row 1: (WS) Sl 1 (selvedge), k2, work in established rib to end.
Row 2: Sl 1 (selvedge), p2, k2, ssk, work in established rib to last 7 sts, k2tog, k2, p3—2 sts dec'd.
Rep the last 2 rows five more times—39 sts rem. Work even in rib, maintaining established slipped selvedge sts, until piece measures 7" (18 cm) from BO, ending with a WS row. Place sts on holder. Make a second sleeve the same as the first, but do not break yarn.

FINISHED SIZE
One size fits all; sleeves about 23" (58.5 cm) long.

YARN
Rowan Kid Classic (70% lambswool, 26% kid mohair, 4% nylon; 153 yd [140 m]/ 50 g): #827 juicy (orange), 4 balls. Yarn distributed by Westminster Fibers.

NEEDLES
Size 7 (4.5 mm): 12" (30-cm) circular (cir) or set of 4 double pointed (dpn). Adjust needle size if necessary to obtain the correct gauge.

NOTIONS
Marker (m); stitch holder; tapestry needle.

GAUGE
20 sts and 22 rows (rounds) = 4" (10 cm) in k3, p3 rib with ribbing slightly stretched.

TURTLENECK

Joining rnd: (RS) Work across 39 sts on needle(s) in established rib, using the backward-loop method (see Glossary), CO 9 sts, with RS of other sleeve facing, work across 39 sts from holder in established rib, CO 9 sts as before—96 sts total. Place m and join for working in the rnd. Work in k3, p3 rib as established until turtleneck measures 8" (20.5 cm) from joining rnd. BO all sts loosely in rib.

FINISHING

Weave in loose ends.

A simple ribbed scarf converts to a shoulder-warming shrug.

WEAR-AS-A-COLLAR SCARF
SALLY MELVILLE

In working on designs for her book, *The Knit Stitch*, Sally Melville discovered that shaping a scarf into something other than a rectangle gives a scarf "something to do." She first made use of a shaped-scarf design—a small triangle with long tails—in the Shape It! Scarf in her book. The piece shown here is an evolution of that design; a larger, broader base with shorter tails. It can be worn as a simple collar tied on the shoulder or like the original scarf—a cowl with tails. Coordinated novelty yarns, used together, add depth and interest to the surface.

FINISHED SIZE
10½" (26.5 cm) at widest point, and 72" (183 cm) long.

YARN
The Collection SRK Ranee (80% polyamide, 20% polyester; 77 yd [70 m]/50 g): #53 brown (A), 1 skein. The Collection SRK Sari (100% polyamide; 104 yd [95 m]/50 g): #603 brown/plum variegated (B), 1 skein. The Collection SRK Persia (80% wool, 10% polyamide, 10% polyester; 49 yd [45 m]/50 g): #603 brown variegated (C), 1 skein. Yarns distributed by S. R. Kertzer.

NEEDLES
Size 10½ (6.5 mm). Adjust needle size if necessary to obtain the correct gauge.

NOTIONS
Tapestry needle.

GAUGE
10 sts and 24 rows = 4" (10 cm) in garter st after hard steam pressing.

> **NOTE**
> ❖ Use the backward-loop method (see Glossary) for all cast-ons. To avoid enlarging the loops, do not stretch the yarn as you cast on—when knitting a cast-on stitch, do not pull the right needle away from the left needle before working the next stitch; try to keep the needles very close together at all times.

SCARF

[CO 1 st with A, CO 1 st with B] 18 times—36 sts. Turn work and knit 1 row with A. Cont as foll:
Row 1: CO 1 with C, CO 1 with A, knit to end with C—38 sts.
Row 2: CO 1 with B, CO 1 with C, knit to end with B—40 sts.
Row 3: CO 1 with A, CO 1 with B, knit to end with A—42 sts.
Rep Rows 1–3 eleven more times—108 sts.
Row 37: [CO 1 with C, CO 1 with A] 3 times, knit to end with C—114 sts.
Row 38: [CO 1 with B, CO 1 with C] 3 times, knit to end with B—120 sts.
Row 39: [CO 1 with A, CO 1 with B] 3 times, knit to end with A—126 sts.
Rep Rows 37–39 three more times—180 sts. Knit 1 row each with C, B, and A, in that order, until piece measures 3½" (9 cm) above last CO, or until you are about to run out of yarn. Work 1 more row with the next yarn in sequence, then BO on next row with the foll yarn in sequence.

FINISHING

Weave in loose ends. With iron on wool setting, using steam or a damp pressing cloth, press heavily on both sides.

GARTER-STITCH WRAP

CATHERINE LOWE

Catherine Lowe discovered the shape for her wrap while she was ironing napkins. She had been pondering how to create a wrap that would be balanced and drape gracefully, but wouldn't be heavy or awkward to wear. As she folded a napkin to put it away, she began playing with it, folding it in half from corner to corner to form triangles. When she unfolded it, she found that she had a square made of interlocking triangles, a napkin folded as if it were being prepared for a piece of origami. The folds in the napkin became the basis for her design—knitted triangles ingeniously joined together to form a square. The opening, a slit in the square from a corner to the center, is formed by leaving one pair of triangles unconnected.

STITCH GUIDE

Single Twisted Chain Stitch Selvedges: (used along the edges of garter st) Slip (sl) the first st purlwise through the back loop (tbl) with yarn in front (wyif), knit last st.

Single Twisted Slipstitch Selvedges: (used along edges of St st) On RS rows, sl the first st pwise tbl wyif, knit last st; on WS rows, sl the first st knitwise with yarn in back (wyib), purl last st.

Twisted Purl Center Double Decrease: (worked on WS) Sl 2 sts tog as if to p2tog tbl wyif, p1, p2sso—2 sts dec'd.

NOTE

✤ The shawl is worked in four separate garter-stitch triangles with single twisted chain stitch selvedges (see Stitch Guide).

✤ Each triangle is worked from center of base.

✤ Work all yarn joins within the knitted fabric, and not at the edges, either by splicing the yarns as they are joined or by weaving the tails invisibly into the wrong side of the fabric using a duplicate stitch.

✤ All stitch counts include yarnovers.

FINISHED SIZE

56" (142 cm) square, after blocking.

YARN

Habu Textiles Fuwa Fuwa (40% mohair, 33% Merino wool, 27% silk; 3000 yd [2743 m]/567 g): #1 (pale olive), one cone.

NEEDLES

Size 6 (4 mm): four 47" (120-cm) or longer circular (cir) for working shawl. Size 7 (4.5 mm): straight, double pointed, or cir of any length for working BO *only*. Optional size 5 (3.75 mm) or smaller: straight, double pointed, or cir of any length for working CO *only*. Adjust needle size if necessary to obtain the correct gauge.

NOTIONS

Tapestry needle; point protectors (4 pair); 22 markers (8 ordinary closed markers to slip onto the needle between sts, and 14 removable markers or coilless safety pins for marking individual sts).

GAUGE

In garter st, 22 sts and 44 rows = 4" (10 cm) before blocking; and 20 sts and 40 rows = 4" (10 cm) after blocking. In stockinette st (St st), 22 sts and 32 rows = 4" (10 cm) before blocking; and 20 sts and 32 rows = 4" (10 cm) after blocking.

TIP 1:

If you find that slipping the center st markers becomes tiresome, you may remove these markers if you are confident that you can recognize the center st and its companion yo, and remember to work a yo after the center st is worked on each row.

SCARF

TRIANGLE 1

CO 5 sts firmly, using the optional smaller needle if desired, and leaving an 8 to 10" (20-cm to 25-cm) tail. Mark the first and last sts by placing removable markers or coilless safety pins around the CO chain bet the first 2 and last 2 sts; these markers will be left in the work until the final steps of construction.

Foundation Row 1: (RS) K1, *yo, k1; rep from * to end—9 sts.

Foundation Row 2: Sl 1 pwise tbl wyif (single twisted chain st selvedge, see Stitch Guide), being careful not to lose the beg yo, take yarn bet needles to back of work, *k1tbl, k1; rep from *—9 sts on needle. (**Note:** Each k1tbl is worked in a yo of the previous row.)

Foundation Row 3: Sl 1 pwise tbl wyif, take yarn to back of work, k2, yo, k3, yo, k3—11 sts.

Foundation Row 4: Sl 1 pwise tbl wyif, take yarn bet needles to back of work, k2, k1tbl, k3, k1tbl, k3—11 sts. (**Note:** As with Foundation Row 2, each k1tbl is worked in the yo of the previous row.)

This completes the foundation section of the triangle. Cont as foll:

Row 1: (RS) Sl 1 pwise tbl wyif, take yarn to back of work, k4, place marker (pm), k1 (center st), pm, yo, k3, yo, k2—13 sts.

To distinguish between the RS and WS of the work, mark the side of the work facing you with a marker or piece of scrap yarn to indicate that it is the RS.

Row 2: Sl 1 pwise tbl wyif, take yarn to back of work, k1, k1tbl in yo of previous row, k3, k1tbl in yo of previous row, sl m, k1 (center st), sl m, yo, k3, yo, k2—15 sts.

Row 3: Sl 1 pwise tbl wyif, take yarn to back of work, k1, k1tbl in yo of previous row, k3, k1tbl in yo of previous row, sl m, k1 (center st), sl m, yo, k5, yo, k2—17 sts.

Row 4: Sl 1 pwise tbl wyif, take yarn to back of work, k1, k1tbl in yo of previous row, k5, k1tbl in yo of previous row, sl m, k1 (center st), sl m, yo, k5, yo, k2—19 sts.

Row 5: Sl 1 pwise tbl wyif, take yarn to back of work, k1, k1tbl in yo of previous row, knit to 1 st before first m (yo of previous row), k1tbl in yo of previous row, sl m, k1 (center st), sl m, yo, knit to last 2 sts, yo, k2—2 sts inc'd.

Row 6: Rep Row 5—2 sts inc'd.

Rep Rows 5 and 6 to work the triangle shape. Each pair of rows will add 4 sts. Even though Rows 5 and 6 are worked identically, you must work both rows of the pair before the number of sts on each side of the center st are the same again.

Work until Row 182 has been completed—375 sts.

Row 183: (RS, non-increase row) Sl 1 pwise tbl wyif, take yarn to back of work, k1, k1tbl in yo of previous row, knit to last st before first m (yo of previous row), k1tbl in yo, sl m, k1 (center st), sl m, knit to end—375 sts.

Place a marker after the 192nd st, counting from the beg of a RS row (this should be the 4th st after the center st). Remove markers on either side of the center st. Cut yarn, leaving a 5½-yd (5-m) tail to be used for finishing the shawl. Leave the sts on the needle.

Lay piece RS up on a flat surface, and form a triangle with the selvedges across the bottom of the triangle, and bending the cable portion of the cir needle to divide the live sts into the two rem sides, with the center st at the top point of the triangle. The first st of the row just completed should be at the lower right, and the last st with the yarn tail at the lower left. Label this triangle as Triangle 1, and mark sts as foll: first st of RS row, 1A; marker placed after 192nd st, 1C; last st of RS row, 1D. (See diagram on page 94.) Set aside Triangle 1.

TRIANGLE 2

Work as for Triangle 1 until Row 183 has been completed—375 sts. Place markers after the 183rd and 192nd sts, counting from the beg of a RS row, to mark the center 9 sts of the row. Remove markers on either side of the center st. Cut yarn, leaving a 5½-yd (5-m) tail to be used for finishing the shawl. Leave the sts on the needle.

Lay piece RS up on a flat surface, and form a triangle with the selvedges across the bottom of the triangle, and bending the cable portion of the cir needle to divide the live sts into the two rem sides, with the center st at the top point of the triangle. The first st of the row just completed should be at the lower right, and the last stitch with the yarn tail at the lower left. Label this triangle as Triangle 2, and mark sts as foll: first st of RS row, 2A; marker placed after 183rd st, 2B; marker placed after the 192nd st, 2C; last st of RS row, 2D. Set aside Triangle 2.

TRIANGLE 3

Work as for Triangle 1 until Row 183 has been completed—375 sts. Place markers after the 183rd and 192nd sts, counting from the beg of a RS row, to mark the center 9 sts of the row, exactly as for Triangle 2. Remove markers on either side of the center st. Cut yarn, leaving a 5½-yd (5-m) tail to be used for finishing the shawl. Leave the sts on the needle. Label this triangle as Triangle 3, and mark sts as for Triangle 2, identifying them as foll: first st of RS row, 3A; marker placed after 183rd st, 3B; marker placed after the 192nd st, 3C; last st of RS row, 3D. Set aside Triangle 3.

TIP 2:

With or without the markers around the center st, the rhythm of the rows becomes easy and regular. Work the selvedge st as sl 1 pwise tbl wyif, k1, k1tbl in the yo of the previous row, knit to next yo, k1tbl in the yo, k1 (center st), yo, knit to last 2 sts of the row, yo, k2.

TRIANGLE 4

Work as for Triangle 1 until Row 183 has been completed—375 sts. Place a marker after the 183rd st, counting from the beg of a RS row, (this should be the 5th st before the center st). Remove markers on either side of the center st. Do not cut yarn. Leave sts on the needle. Label this triangle as Triangle 4, and mark sts, identifying them as foll: first st of RS row, 4A; marker placed after 183rd st, 4B; last st of RS row, 4D.

ASSEMBLY

Join Triangles 3 and 4: Place Triangles 3 and 4 tog with WS facing each other, and matching point 4A with 3D, and point 4B with 3C. Position the needles so the sts of Triangle 4 are on the near needle, and those of Triangle 3 are on the far needle. With size 7 (4.5-mm) needle and using the three-needle method (see Glossary) and the yarn tail from 3D, BO 182 sts tog on the RS, working from 4A/3D to 4B/3C. **Note:** Work the BO firmly and evenly, but not so tightly that the seam puckers, nor so loosely that the join ripples and is unstable. If necessary, use a larger or smaller needle so that you can work the BO comfortably at a gauge that is consistent with that of the triangle.

When St #182 has been BO and St #183 rem on right needle, work as foll: Leave marker 4B on the needle for Triangle 4, and transfer the last st from the BO to needle 4, placing it in front of marker 4B. Drop the yarn tail to the WS. Transfer marker 3C to needle 4, then transfer the next 9 sts from needle 3 to needle 4, and finally transfer marker 3B to needle 4. Secure the ends of needle 4 so the sts and markers will not fall off—183 sts rem on needle 3; 202 sts on needle 4: 192 sts from Triangle 4, 1 st from BO bet Triangles 3 and 4, and 9 center sts from Triangle 3.

Join Triangles 2 and 3: Place Triangles 2 and 3 tog with WS facing each other, and matching point 3A with 2D, and point 3B with 2C. Position needles so the sts of Triangle 3 are on the near needle, and those of Triangle 2 are on the far needle. With size 7 (4.5-mm) needle and using the three-needle method and the yarn tail from 2D, BO 182 sts tog on the RS, working from 3A/2D to 3B/2C. When St #182 has been BO and St #183 rem on the right needle, work as foll: Remove what was used to secure the sts and markers of needle 4, transfer the last st from the BO to needle 4, placing it next to marker 3B. Drop the yarn tail to the WS. Transfer marker 2C to needle 4, then transfer the next 9 sts from needle 2 to needle 4, and finally transfer marker 2B to needle 4. Secure the ends of needle 4 so the sts and markers will not fall off—183 sts on needle 2; 212 sts on needle 4: 192 sts from Triangle 4, 1 st from BO bet Triangles 3 and 4, 9 center sts from Triangle 3, 1 st from BO between Triangles 2 and 3, and 9 center sts from Triangle 2.

Join Triangles 1 and 2: Place Triangles 1 and 2 tog with WS facing each other, and matching point 2A with 1D, and point 2B with 1C. Position needles so the sts of Triangle 2 are on the near needle, and those of Triangle 1 are on the far needle. With size 7 (4.5-mm) needle and using the three-needle method and the yarn tail from 1D, BO 182 sts tog on the RS, working from 2A/1D to 2B/1C.

When St #182 has been BO and St #183 rem on the right needle, work as foll: Remove what was used to secure the sts and markers of needle 4, transfer the last st from the BO to needle 4, placing it next to marker 2B. Drop the yarn tail to the WS. Transfer marker 1C to needle 4, then transfer all the rem sts from needle 1 to needle 4—405 sts: 192 sts from Triangle 4, 1 st from BO between Triangles 3 and 4, 9 center sts from Triangle 3, 1 st from BO between Triangles 2 and 3, 9 center sts from Triangle 2, 1 st from BO between Triangles 1 and 2, and 192 sts of Triangle 1.

STABILIZE THE OPENING

Hold the work so that the WS of shawl is facing and point 4D with the working yarn attached at the beg of the row. *Next row:* (WS) Sl 1 pwise tbl wyif, take yarn to back of work, knit to 1 st before marker 4B, sl the next 3 sts to right needle removing markers, then sl these 3 sts back to left needle and work them tog as purl center double dec (see Stitch Guide), knit to 1 st before marker 3B, removing markers work the next 3 sts as purl center double dec, knit to 1 st before marker 2B, work the next 3 sts as purl center double dec, knit to end—399 sts rem. Place removable markers around the base of the selvedge st at each end of the row just completed in order to identify these sts later. Do not place the markers through the loops of the sts. On the next row, BO all sts knitwise, working the first st as p1tbl to maintain the selvedge st. Work the BO firmly, using the same size needle used to join the triangles. Secure the last st, but do not cut the yarn.

EDGING

Turn the work so that WS is facing. Using the working yarn from the BO row and one of the main size cir needles, pick up and knit 1 st in the loop of each st in the row below the BO row, beg and ending in the loops of the marked selvedge sts at each end of the row—399 sts. Remove the markers around the selvedge sts. *Next row:* (RS) P1, knit to end. Turn, and work a rolled St st edging with single twisted slip stitch selvedges (see Stitch Guide), beg with a WS row, as foll:
Row 1: (WS) Sl 1 kwise wyib, take yarn to front of work, purl to end.
Row 2: Sl 1 pwise tbl wyif, knit to end.

Rep Rows 1 and 2 twice more—6 rows completed. On the next row (WS), BO all sts kwise, working the first st as p1tbl to maintain selvedge. Secure the last st and cut yarn. The St st edging should roll toward the pick-up row with the purl side out.

FINISHING

Weave in ends from the last BO row along the WS of the BO chain. Weave the ends from each of the three-needle BOs along the WS of shawl using duplicate stitch (see Glossary). Close the CO portion of bottom edge of each triangle as foll: Join the first and last sts of the CO using the yarn end to weave a figure-eight in the CO chain, working first bet the first 2 and then the last 2 marked sts of the CO. Secure the end and weave it invisibly into WS of the knitted fabric. Remove markers from the CO row. Weave in all ends from yarn joins along the WS of the fabric. Remove all rem markers. Block the shawl to about 56" (142 cm) square. Do not remove from the blocking surface until the fabric is thoroughly dry.

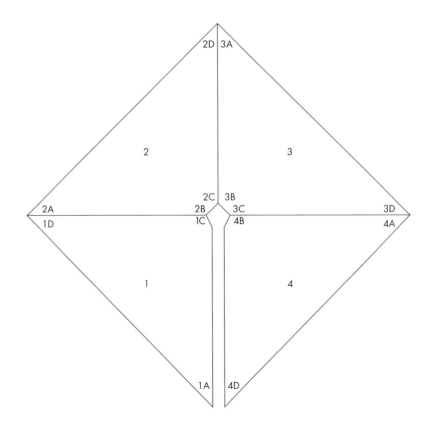

Heading out to a midwinter gala? Running errands in town on a snowy day? Skating upriver through the trees? This down-to-earth scarf will keep you snug whatever you do, and its feminity will make you feel at home in your best dress or add a little class to your practical coat. Ivy Bigelow has chosen a simple, tailored lace pattern, based on the Tilting Block Pattern from *Barbara Walker's Second Treasury of Knitting Patterns*, for a graceful scarf that isn't overly fussy. Says Ivy, "The tweedy, rustic quality of this soft yarn gives the lace a delicious earthiness. And working with an organic cotton-and-wool blend is as good as eating soul food." In an icy blue, this scarf is regal enough for a winter queen.

SCARF

CO 49 sts. Knit 3 rows. Cont as foll:

Rows 1, 3, 5, and 7: (RS) *[K2tog, yo] four times, k8; rep from * two more times, end k1.

Rows 2, 4, 6, and 8: *K9, p7; rep from * to last st, k1.

Rows 9, 11, 13, and 15: K1, *k8, [yo, ssk] four times; rep from *.

Rows 10, 12, 14, and 16: K1, *p7, k9; rep from *.

Rep Rows 1–16 a total of 25 times (400 patt rows). Knit 3 rows. BO all sts.

FINISHING

Weave in loose ends. Block lightly, if desired.

FINISHED SIZE
10" (25.5 cm) wide and 60" (152.5 cm) long, after blocking.

YARN
Green Mountain Spinnery Cotton Comfort (80% wool, 20% organic cotton; 180 yd [165 m]/2 oz [57] g): bluet, 3 skeins.

NEEDLES
Size 6 (4 mm). Adjust needle size if necessary to obtain the correct gauge.

NOTIONS
Tapestry needle.

GAUGE
21 sts and 32 rows = 4" (10 cm) in garter st.

Leigh Radford used a lofty alpaca-blend yarn to make a spectacular oversize shawl. The stitch pattern is simple to work and easy to memorize; the chunky yarn and large crochet hook make it a quick project. It's finished with an edging of single crochet. Wear it with pendant earrings and you have a dressy wrap; wear it curled up in an armchair and you have casual at-home comfort.

NOTE

❖ See Glossary for crochet instructions.

SHAWL

Ch 58.

Row 1: (WS) Work 1 hdc in 2nd ch from hook, then work 1 hdc in each ch to end. Turn.

Row 2: Ch 1, work 1 hdc in each of the next 3 hdc, *ch 5, skip 3 hdc, work 1 hdc in each of the next 5 hdc; rep from *, end by working 1 hdc in each of the last 3 hdc. Turn.

Row 3: Ch 1, work 1 hdc in each of the next 2 hdc, *ch 3, work 1 hdc in ch-5 arch, ch 3, skip 1 hdc, work 1 hdc in each of the next 3 hdc; rep from *, end by working 1 hdc in each of the last 2 hdc. Turn.

Row 4: Ch 1, work 1 hdc in the next hdc, *ch 3, work 1 hdc in ch-3 arch, work 1 hdc in next hdc, work 1 hdc in ch-3 arch, ch 3, skip 1 hdc, work 1 hdc in next hdc; rep from * to end. Turn.

Row 5: Ch 5 (count as 1 dc, ch 2), work 1 hdc in next ch-3 arch, work 1 hdc in each of the next 3 hdc, work 1 hdc in ch-3 arch, *ch 5, work 1 hdc in ch-3 arch, work 1 hdc in each of the next 3 hdc, work 1 hdc in ch-3 arch; rep from *, end by working ch 2, 1 dc in last hdc. Turn.

Row 6: Ch 1, work 1 hdc in dc, ch 3, skip 1 hdc, work 1 hdc in each of the next 3 hdc, *ch 3, work 1 hdc in ch-5 arch, ch 3, skip 1 hdc, work 1 hdc in each of the next 3 hdc; rep from * to final ch-2 arch, end ch 3, work 1 hdc in 3rd or 5th ch at beg of previous row. Turn.

FINISHED SIZE
About 27½" (70 cm) wide and 81" (205.5 cm) long.

YARN
Reynolds Blizzard (65% alpaca, 35% acrylic; 66 yd [60 m]/100 g): #612 light blue, 12 skeins.

NOTIONS
Size P/16 (11.5-mm) crochet hook; tapestry needle.

GAUGE
Not critical for this project.

Row 7: Ch 1, work 1 hdc in next hdc, work 1 hdc in ch-3 arch, ch 3, skip 1 hdc, work 1 sc in next hdc, *ch 3, work 1 hdc in next ch-3 arch, work 1 hdc in next hdc, work 1 hdc in ch-3 arch, ch 3, skip 1 hdc, work 1 hdc in next hdc; rep from * to last ch-3 arch, end ch 3, work 1 hdc in ch-3 arch, work 1 hdc in next hdc. Turn.

Row 8: Ch 1, work 1 hdc in next 2 hdc, *work 1 hdc in ch-3 arch, ch 5, work 1 hdc in ch-3 arch, work 1 hdc in each of next 3 hdc; rep from *, omitting final hdc at end of last rep. Turn.

Rep Rows 3–8 until piece measures about 79" (200.5 cm), ending with Row 8. Cut yarn and fasten off.

FINISHING

Weave in loose ends. Position shawl flat on the floor like a vertical rectangle, RS facing up, and foundation chain across the bottom short side of the rectangle. Rejoin yarn to lower right corner of work with RS facing. Work 1 row of hdc around three sides, ending at the other end of the foundation row. Without cutting the yarn, then work 1 row of sc around all four sides. Cut yarn and weave in ends. Block, if desired.

Use a fine yarn and small crochet hook to convert this pattern into a delicate neck scarf.

There are a variety of ways to make knitted ruffles, and Teva Durham has used a short-row method for her silky ribbon collar. Alternating needle size every few inches emphasized by a subtle rippling effect. If you're adventurous, Teva suggests teaching yourself to knit backward with the right side of the fabric always facing you. This technique takes a bit of practice to do speedily and at an even gauge, but once mastered it makes short-rowing fun—you don't have to keep turning your knitting back and forth.

STITCH GUIDE

Wrap St: (WS) With yarn in front, slip 1 st from left needle to right needle, bring yarn to back between needles in position to purl on WS, return slipped st to left needle.

Knit Wrapped St with Wrap: (RS) Insert right needle tip into both the wrap at the base of the wrapped st and the st itself, then knit them both together.

COLLAR

With smaller needles and using the long-tail method (see Glossary), CO 36 sts.

Row 1: (WS) K3 (neck edge sts), purl to last 2 sts, k2 (shoulder edge sts).

Row 2: Knit.

Rep the last 2 rows two more times—6 rows completed. *Change to larger needles, and work Row 1 once more. Cont in St st, working edge sts in garter st as established, and *at the same time* work short-rows on RS as foll:

Short-row 1: K8, wrap st (see Stitch Guide), turn, purl to last 2 sts, k2.

Short-row 2: K8, knit wrapped st with wrap, k4, wrap st, turn, purl to last 2 sts, k2.

Short-rows 3, 4, and 5: Knit to wrapped st, knit wrapped st with wrap, k4, wrap st, turn, purl to last 2 sts, k2.

Short-row 6: Knit to wrapped st from previous row, wrap st again (2 wraps on same st), turn, purl to last 2 sts, k2.

Short-rows 7, 8, 9, and 10: Knit to 5 sts before wrapped st from previous row, wrap st, turn, purl to last 2 sts, k2.

Change to smaller needles. Knit 1 row across all sts, knitting wrapped sts with their wraps (the wrapped st closest to the neck edge will have 2 wraps to be worked with the st). Continue with smaller needles. Working edge sts in garter st as established, work 6 rows St st, ending with a

FINISHED SIZE
21" (53.5 cm) long at neck edge, and 8" (20.5 cm) at deepest point of ruffle, not including ties.

YARN
Berroco Glace (100% rayon; 75 yd [69 m]/50 g): #2578 workshirt (light blue), 4 balls.

NEEDLES
Size 5 (3.75 mm) and 9 (5.5 mm). Adjust needle size if necessary to obtain the correct gauge.

NOTIONS
Tapestry needle; stitch holder; size H/8 (5-mm) crochet hook.

GAUGE
20 sts and 32 rows = 4" (10 cm) in St st on smaller needles; 16 sts and 24 rows = 4" (10 cm) in St st on larger needles.

RS row. Repeat from * after Row 2 until neck edge measures about 20" (51 cm) from beg, and end having just completed 5 rows of St st with smaller needles. *Next row:* (RS) Knit to last 3 sts (neck edge sts), place last 3 sts on holder—33 sts rem. With WS facing, BO all sts loosely. Cut yarn.

FINISHING

With RS facing, rejoin yarn to CO edge, just below the 3 neck edge sts. With crochet hook, work 1 row single crochet (sc; see Glossary for crochet instructions) along the CO, outer, and BO edges, working 1 sc for every st along CO and BO edges, 1 sc into the selvedge st of each row worked with larger needles, and 1 sc into every *other* row for rows worked with smaller needles, ending just below the 3 held neck edge sts. Cut yarn, leaving an 8-yd (8-m) tail for working tie, and fasten off last st. ***Ties***: With RS facing, return 3 sts from holder to smaller needles, ready to work a RS row. Using long tail, work these 3 sts in garter st until tie measures 6" (15 cm). BO all sts. Rejoin yarn at other end of collar with RS facing, and pick up and knit 3 sts from other neck edge to correspond to position of first tie. Work second tie the same as the first. Weave in loose ends. Steam lightly.

A garter stitch tie makes a simple closure for this silky collar, but a vintage button and crocheted loop would work equally well.

Clever use of short-rows makes the outer edges of this scarf longer than the center "spine," creating a ruffle effect. Amanda Blair Brown made her scarf reversible by using smooth stockinette stitch on one side of the center line and textured reverse stockinette on the other. Another way to work this scarf might be to make each side of the ruffle in a different color.

STITCH GUIDE

Wrap and Turn (w&t): Slip next st to right needle as if to purl, bring yarn to front between the needles (do not bring yarn over needle), return slipped st to left needle, bring yarn to back between the needles, turn work—1 st wrapped.

Knit Wrap and Wrapped Stitch Together (kwtog): Insert tip of right needle under the wrap as if to knit, then into the wrapped stitch, and knit both loops together (the wrap and the stitch).

SCARF

CO 22 sts. Work set-up row as foll: Sl 1 as if to knit (kwise) with yarn in back (wyib), k10, p11. Change to patt and work as foll:

Row 1: Sl 1 kwise wyib, k8, w&t, purl to end.
Row 2: Sl 1 kwise wyib, k6, w&t, purl to end.
Row 3: Sl 1 kwise wyib, k4, w&t, purl to end.
Row 4: Sl 1 kwise wyib, k4, [kwtog, k1] 3 times, purl to end.

Rep Rows 1–4 until piece measures 86" (218.5 cm) along the unruffled centerline, or desired length. BO all sts.

FINISHING

Weave in loose ends. Block lightly.

FINISHED SIZE
4½" (11.5 cm) wide (with edges unrolled) and 86" (218.5 cm) long, measured along centerline.

YARN
Classic Elite Premiere (50% pima cotton, 50% Tencel®; 108 yd [99 m]/50 g): #5216 natural, 4 skeins.

NEEDLES
Size 6 (4 mm). Adjust needle size if necessary to obtain the correct gauge.

NOTIONS
Tapestry needle.

GAUGE
20 sts and 34 rows = 4" (10 cm) in St st.

The combination of an open crochet stitch with pearly beads imparts a vintage look to this romantic, dressy scarf. Lily Chin has been incorporating beads into her knitted and crocheted designs for over a decade. She particularly likes the pairing of openwork and solid areas in this crochet pattern. The beads provide a bit of heft to the soft Merino yarn, encouraging its elegant drape and adding a subtle glimmer to the smooth fiber. The beading is confined to the ends of the scarf, so once you've worked the first few inches of each scarf half, the rest is a breeze.

STITCH GUIDE

Bring up Bead (BUB): Slide a bead up the yarn strand close to the hook. Beads are introduced on WS rows and will lie on the RS of the work, on the yarn strand behind a sc or dc.

Lace Shell: *Sc, ch 2, skip the next 2 sts or ch, dc in next st, ch 2, skip 2 sts or ch; rep from * as instructed, usually ending with a sc to finish and balance the lace shell.

Beaded single crochet (Bsc): Draw up a loop in next st, BUB, yarn around hook and draw through both loops on hook to complete st.

Beaded double crochet (Bdc): Yarn around hook, draw up a loop in next st, [BUB, yarn around hook and draw through 2 loops on hook] twice to complete st.

Beaded Shell: (Dc, bdc, dc, bdc, dc) all in same st.

FINISHED SIZE
7" (18 cm) wide and 40" (101.5 cm) long.

YARN
Gems Opal Sport Weight (100% Merino superwash; 225 yd [206 m]/100 g): #01 champagne, 2 skeins. Yarn distributed by Louet Sales.

HOOK
Size G/7 (4.5-mm) crochet hook. Adjust hook size if necessary to obtain the correct gauge.

NOTIONS
Tapestry needle; bead-stringing needle; about 236 size 6 glass seed beads (shown in color #343 from Toho Shoji).

GAUGE
1 shell st = 1" (2.5 cm) wide.

NOTES
❖ Pre-string beads onto yarn before working. Pre-string about half the beads and work the first section; then pre-string the remainder of the beads for second section.
❖ See Glossary for crochet instructions.

FIRST SCARF HALF

Very loosely, ch 45.

Row 1: (WS) Bsc in second ch from hook, *sc in next ch, bsc in next ch; rep from *—44 sts.

Row 2 and all RS rows: Ch 5 (counts as dc and ch 2) and turn, skip first 3 sts or ch, work lace shell across, working last shell as sc in next st, ch 2, skip next 2 sts, dc in last st.

Row 3: Ch 1 and turn, sc in first dc, *skip 2 ch, work beaded shell all in next sc, skip 2 ch, sc in next dc, ch 2, skip 2 ch, dc in next sc, ch 2, skip 2 ch, sc in next dc; rep from *, working last rep as ch 2, skip 2 ch, work beaded shell all in next sc, sc in third ch of 5-st turning ch instead of in a dc—4 beaded shells alternating with 3 lace shells.

Row 5: Ch 1 and turn, sc in first dc, *ch 2, skip 2 ch, dc in next sc, ch 2, skip 2 ch, sc in next dc, skip 2 ch, work beaded shell in next sc, skip 2 ch, sc in next dc; rep from *, two more times ch 2, skip 2 ch, dc in next sc, ch 2, skip 2 ch, sc in third ch of 5-st turning ch instead of in a dc—3 beaded shells alternating with 4 lace shells.

Rows 6–14: Rep Rows 2–5 two more times, then work Row 2 once more.

Row 15: Ch 1 and turn, sc in first dc, [ch 2, skip 2 ch, dc in next sc, ch 2, skip 2 ch, sc in next dc] 2 times, skip 2 ch, work beaded shell in next sc, skip 2 ch, sc in next dc, ch 2, skip 2 ch, dc in next sc, ch 2, skip 2 ch, sc in next dc, skip 2 ch, work beaded shell in next sc, skip 2 ch, sc in next dc, [ch 2, skip 2 ch, dc in next sc, ch 2, skip 2 ch, sc in next dc] 2 times, working last sc in third ch of 5-st turning ch instead of a dc—2 lace shells at each side, and 2 beaded shells with a lace shell bet them at center.

Row 17: Ch 1 and turn, sc in first dc, [ch 2, skip 2 ch, dc in next sc, ch 2, skip 2 ch, sc in next dc] 3 times, work beaded shell in next sc, skip 2 ch, sc in next dc, [ch 2, skip 2 ch, dc in next sc, ch 2, skip 2 ch, sc in next dc] 3 times, working last sc in third ch of 5-st turning ch instead of a dc—1 beaded shell in center with 3 lace shells on either side.

Row 18: Rep Row 2.

Row 19: Ch 1 and turn, sc in first dc, *ch 2, skip 2 ch, dc in next sc, ch 2, skip 2 ch, sc in next dc; rep from *, working last sc in third ch of 5-st turning ch instead of a dc—7 lace shells.

Rep Rows 18 and 19 until piece meas 20" (51 cm) from beg, ending with Row 19. Cut yarn and fasten off last st.

SECOND SCARF HALF

Work as for first half, ending with RS Row 18. Cut yarn, leaving a long tail for seaming, and fasten off last st.

FINISHING

Block pieces to finished measurements. Using the long tail from the second scarf half, sew the last rows tog at center of scarf; beaded shells will be at each end of assembled scarf. *Edging*: With RS facing, join yarn to edge of scarf at seam. Work a row of sc evenly spaced around the entire scarf, working 3 sc in each corner. Join with a slip stitch to first sc at beg of edging. Cut yarn and fasten off last st. Weave in loose ends.

PAM ALLEN

Not exactly a scarf and not quite a shawl, this easy-to-make capelet slips over the head to keep your neck and shoulders warm. Worked in a slightly fuzzy nylon/wool blend, the capelet drapes and moves gracefully. A high, fitted neck and deep ruffle give it a slight Victorian feel, as do the separate "sleeves" that fit easily over the arms and end at the finger line.

NOTE

❖ Ruffle is picked up and worked downward after the capelet is completed.

CAPELET

With 29" (70-cm) cir needle, CO 154 sts. Place marker (pm) and join for beg of round (rnd), being careful not to twist sts. K77 sts for front, pm, knit to end of rnd. Work in St st (knit every rnd) for 11 more rnds. *Dec rnd:* *K2, k2tog, knit to 4 sts before next marker (m), ssk, k2, slip m; rep from * once more—4 sts dec'd; 150 sts rem. Work 10 rnds even. Rep dec rnd—46 sts rem. Work 8 rnds even. Rep dec rnd—142 sts rem. Work 6 rnds even. Rep dec rnd—138 sts rem. Work 4 rnds even. Rep dec rnd—134 sts rem. Work 2 rnds even. Rep dec rnd—130 sts rem. Work dec rnd *every* rnd 8 more times—98 sts rem; piece should measure about 9¾" (24.5 cm) from beg. **Shape shoulders**: Working St st in rows (knit on RS, purl on WS) on 49 front sts only, BO 6 sts at beg of next 4 rows—25 front sts rem. Place front sts on holder. Rejoin yarn to back sts with RS facing. Working back and forth in St st on 49 back sts, BO 6 sts at beg of next 4 rows—25 back sts rem. Place sts on holder. Turn capelet inside out and with yarn threaded on a tapestry needle, sew BO sts tog at each shoulder. **Collar**: Place 50 sts for front and back on 16" (40-cm) cir needle. With RS facing, join yarn at shoulder and pm for beg of rnd. Work in St st in rnds until collar measures 6" (15 cm). BO all sts loosely. **Ruffle:** Beg at side, with longer cir needle and RS facing, pick up and knit 1 st in the first CO st at bottom edge of capelet, *yo, pick up and knit 1 st in next CO st; rep from * to end—308 sts.

FINISHED SIZE
Capelet: 44" (112 cm) circumference just above ruffle and 14¼" (36 cm) long from bottom edge of ruffle to top of shoulders with bottom edge unrolled. Sleeves: 9" (23 cm) circumference at upper edge, 8" (20.5 cm) circumference at wrist, and 19" (48.5 cm) long.

YARN
Berroco Furz (50% nylon, 25% wool, 25% acrylic; 90 yd [83 m]/50 g): #3877 teal, 6 balls for capelet, 2 balls for sleeves.

NEEDLES
Size 10 (6 mm): 29" (70-cm) and 16" (40-cm) circular (cir) for capelet; size 10 (6 mm): set of 5 double pointed (dpn) for sleeves. Adjust needle size if necessary to obtain the correct gauge.

NOTIONS
Markers (m); stitch holder; tapestry needle.

GAUGE
14 sts and 23 rnds = 4" (10 cm) in St st worked in the rnd.

Place m and join. Work St st in rnds until ruffle measures 3¾" (9.5 cm) from pick-up rnd (bottom edge will roll up slightly when finished). BO all sts loosely. Weave in loose ends. Block lightly on WS with steam iron held 1" (2.5 cm) above fabric.

SLEEVES

With dpn, CO 32 sts. Divide sts evenly on four needles, pm, and join for working in the rnd, being careful not to twist sts. Work in St st until piece measures 6" (15 cm) from beg. *Dec rnd*: K1, k2tog, knit to last 3 sts, ssk, k1—2 sts dec'd; 30 sts rem. Work even until piece measures 12" (30.5 cm) from beg. Rep dec rnd—28 sts rem. Work even until piece measures 19" (48.5 cm) from beg. BO all sts. Work second sleeve the same as the first.

FINISHING

Weave in ends.

For added panache, pin a couple of knitted roses to the capelet—instructions are on page 122.

NOT-SO-PLAIN GEOMETRIC SCARF

PAULA JENNE

For Paula Jenne, there is something magical in knitting—the way you make the fabric stitch by stitch and shape it at the same time. As Paula knits along, she makes decisions about color, size, and embellishments. In this scarf, she added pockets for cocooning in her drafty old New England home on subzero winter nights when "I loathe to poke a finger out from my swaddling to grab a tissue or the remote." Paula's scarf with its lively arrangement of colors and subtle embellishments of beads and striped cording will keep your neck—and your hands—warm. Paula hopes knitters will be inspired by her pattern to reinterpret and reinvent it for other versions.

SCARF

With larger needles and dark olive, CO 41 sts. Work St st for 8 rows, ending with a WS row.

Rows 1–42: Work Triangle Block chart (page 115), using dark olive for A (plain squares) and orange for B (X squares), in St st intarsia (twisting yarns at the color joins to prevent leaving holes). This is Triangle Block 1.

Rows 43–48: With blue-purple, work 6 rows St st with blue-purple.

Rows 49–90: Work Triangle Block chart, using light green for A (plain squares) and dark olive for B (X squares). This is Triangle Block 2.

Rows 91–96: With blue-purple, work 6 rows St st.

Rows 97–105: Work Checkerboard chart (page 115), using light green for A (plain squares) and orange for B (X squares) in two-color stranded St st. This is Checkerboard 1.

Rows 106–111: With blue-purple, work 6 rows St st, beg with a WS row, and ending with a RS row.

Row 112: With burgundy, purl 1 row on WS.

Rows 113–154: Work Triangle Block chart, using burgundy for A and light green for B. This is Triangle Block 3.

Rows 155–160: With blue-purple, work 6 rows St st.

Rows 161–198: Work Nine Patch chart (page 117) using colors shown in St st intarsia; the checkerboard motif in the center may be worked in two-color stranded St st if desired.

Rows 199–204: With blue-purple, work 6 rows St st.

Rows 205–246: Work Triangle Block chart, using dark olive for A and burgundy for B. This is Triangle Block 4.

Rows 247–252: With blue-purple, work 6 rows St st.

FINISHED SIZE
7½" (19 cm) wide and 52" (132 cm) long.

YARN
Jaeger Extra Fine Merino DK (100% Merino; 137 yd [125 m]/50 g): #988 alpine (dark olive), #945 black currant (blue-purple), #987 cypress (light green), #979 tango (orange), #984 violet, #920 wineberry (burgundy), 1 ball each. Yarn distributed by Westminster Fibers. **Note:** Almost every inch of dark olive, blue-purple, light green, and orange were used. You may want to buy two skeins of these colors for safety's sake—the leftovers would make wonderful mittens!

NEEDLES
Size 7 (4.5 mm): double pointed (dpn) or 24" (60-cm) circular (cir) for scarf. Size 6 (4 mm) or size 7 (4.5 mm): 2 dpn for filler cord covering. Adjust needle size if necessary to obtain the correct gauge.

NOTIONS
Stitch holder; size F/6 (4-mm) crochet hook; tapestry needle; smaller needle for applying beads (if other needle will not fit through the bead holes); size 6° Czech glass beads, ruby (60), violet (24), and blue-gray (24); 2 yd (2 m) 5/32" (4-mm) filler cord; Delta Jewel glue for securing beads after sewing; ¾ yd (meter) lining fabric 45" (110 cm) or wider (optional); sewing needle and matching thread for attaching lining (optional).

GAUGE
22 sts and 30 rows = 4" (10 cm) in St st.

Rows 253–261: Work Checkerboard chart, using dark olive for A and orange for B. This is Checkerboard 2.

Rows 262–267: With blue-purple, work 6 rows St st, beg with a WS row, and ending with a RS row.

Row 268: With light green, purl 1 row on WS.

Rows 269–310: Work Triangle Block chart, using light green for A and dark olive for B. This is Triangle Block 5.

Rows 311–316: With blue-purple, work 6 rows St st.

Rows 317–358: Work Triangle Block chart, using orange for A and light green for B. This is Triangle Block 6.

Rows 359–364: With blue-purple, work 6 rows St st.

Rows 365–373: Work Checkerboard chart, using dark olive for A and burgundy for B. This is Checkerboard 3.

Work 8 rows St st with blue-purple, beg and ending with a WS row. BO all sts.

EMBROIDERY

Diagonal running stitch lines: With yarn threaded on a tapestry needle, work lines of diagonal running sts along the diagonal color change in each Triangle Block, as shown in illustration on page 116. Working from right to left, insert the needle into the center of the first st and under the left leg of the same st, then insert it into the center of the next st to the left, one row up, along the color change line, and take it under the left leg of that st. Cont until the entire line is completed. Use the following colors for each Triangle Block: #1 dark olive, #2 blue-purple, #3 dark olive, #4 light green, #5 orange, and #6 dark olive. *Horizontal running stitch lines:* With violet threaded on a tapestry needle, work lines of horizontal running stitch as shown in illustration on page 116 on the first and last row of each blue-purple stripe. Working from right to left, *insert the needle under the right leg of the 'V' of first stitch on right, then through the right legs of several stitches along the row as shown in the illustration. Pull the yarn through and repeat from *. *Backstitch:* Working from right to left, bring needle out from wrong to right side between the first two knitted stitches you want to cover. *Insert the needle at the right edge of the first stitch on the right and bring it out at the left edge of the second stitch. Insert the needle again between the first two stitches and bring it out between the next two stitches to be covered. Repeat from *. With yarn threaded on a tapestry needle, work lines of backstitch in the following six places with the color indicated: Triangle Block 2: Row 3, using violet. Blue-purple stripe below Checkerboard 2: Fifth row of stripe, using orange. Blue-purple stripe above Checkerboard 2: Second row of stripe, using orange. Triangle Block 5: Row 42, using orange. Triangle Block 6: Row 42, using burgundy. Checkerboard 3: Rows 1 and 9, using burgundy.

Diagonal running stitch

Horizontal running stitch

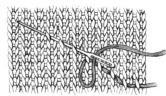

Backstitch

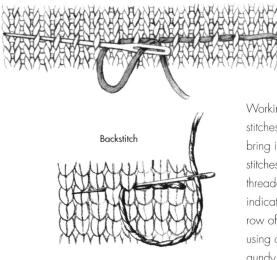

Checkerboard

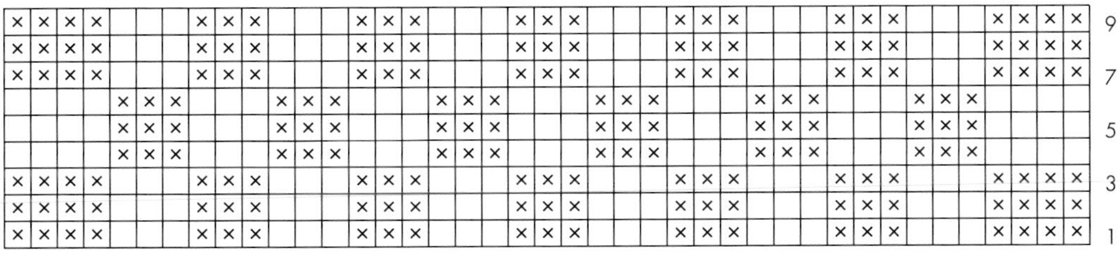

9
7
5
3
1

Triangle Block

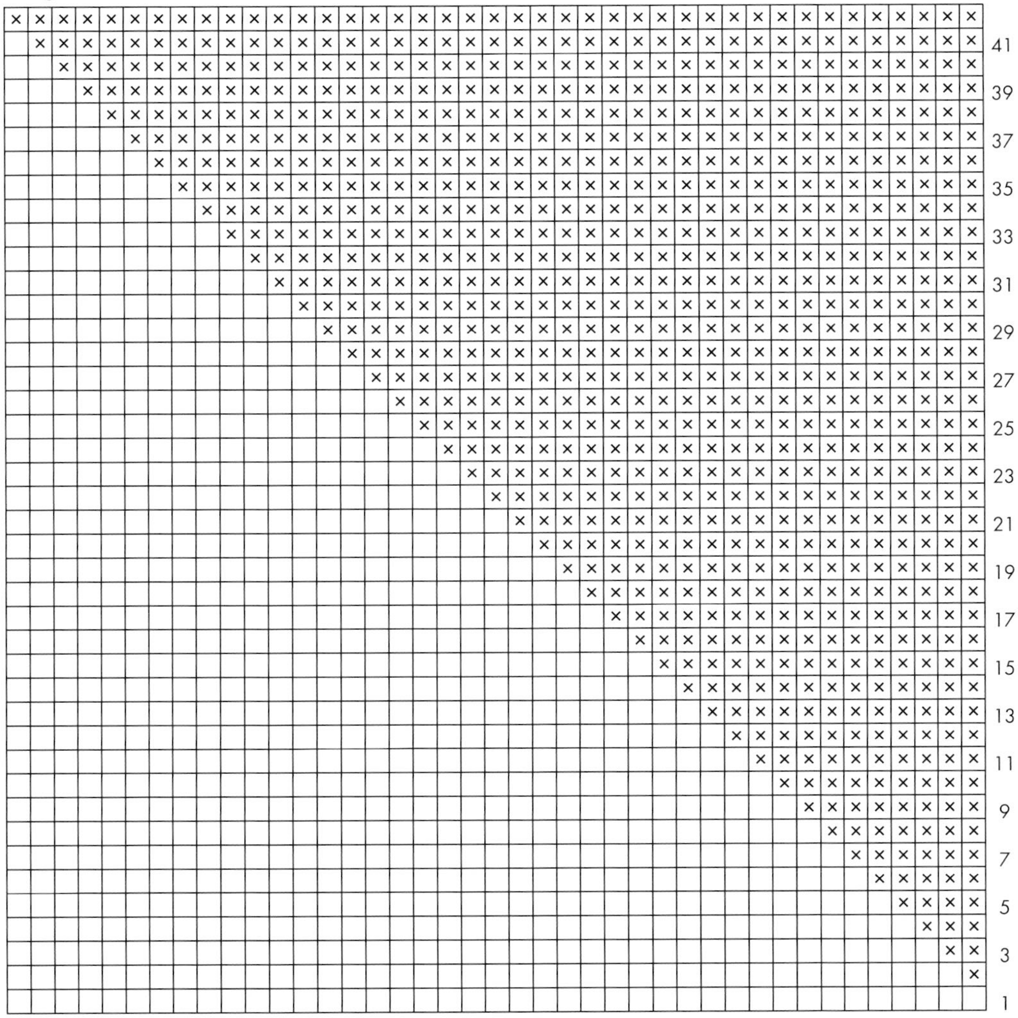

41
39
37
35
33
31
29
27
25
23
21
19
17
15
13
11
9
7
5
3
1

☐ color A*

☒ color B*

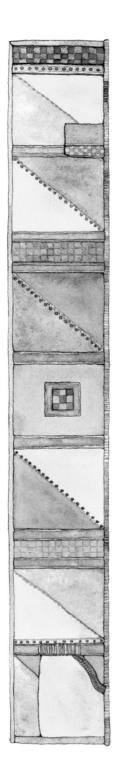

BEADS

The glass beads are applied by stitching (use a smaller needle, if necessary), then glued in place, in the foll five places with the colors indicated: **Triangle Block 2:** Row 2, every 3rd st, violet beads with blue-purple yarn. **Triangle Block 3:** Along the 2nd st above the diagonal line, ruby beads with burgundy yarn. **Triangle Block 4:** Along the 2nd st below the diagonal line, ruby beads with orange yarn. **Triangle Block 5:** Along the 2nd st below the diagonal line, blue-gray beads with dark olive yarn. **Blue-purple stripe below Checkerboard 3:** Third row of stripe, ruby beads with burgundy yarn.

SHAPED POCKET

With RS facing, larger needles, and light green, pick up and knit the first 30 sts along Row 1 of Triangle Block 1. Work St st for 25 rows, beg and ending with a WS row. *Shape pocket:* BO 1 st at beg of next 14 RS rows—16 sts rem. Change to blue-purple and knit 1 row. Place sts on a holder. *Shaped edge facing:* With larger needles, RS facing, and blue-purple, pick up and knit 26 sts along shaped edge of pocket. Work 3 rows St st, beg and ending with a WS row, purl 1 row on RS (turning ridge), knit 1 row. Change to orange and work 2 rows St st. BO all sts. *Top edge facing:* Return 16 held sts to needle with RS facing. With blue-purple, pick up and knit 5 sts along the selvedge of shaped edge facing, beg at turning ridge, knit across the 16 sts for top of pocket—21 sts. Join light green, and work as foll:

Row 1: (WS) *P1 blue-purple, p1 light green; rep from * to last st, p1 blue-purple.
Row 2: *K1 blue-purple, k1, light green; rep from * to last st, k1 blue-purple.
Rep Rows 1 and 2 once more. BO all sts on next row with blue-purple. Sew straight left side of pocket to Triangle 1. Sew across top edge facing, aligning top of facing with top of blue-purple stripe. On the shaped edge facing, work horizontal running stitch lines with burgundy on the first and third St st rows (the row just above the pick-up row, and the row just below the turning ridge). With dark olive, work a line of backstitches over every other st in the second St st row. Fold facing along turning ridge and slip-stitch to WS of pocket. Weave in ends. Leave rem short pocket side unattached for now; it will be joined to the layer below when the edging is applied.

PATCH POCKET

The patch pocket is worked upside-down when the scarf is held in the direction of knitting, but this will allow the pocket to face the right way up when the scarf is draped around the wearer's neck. Turn the scarf upside-down with RS facing you so that Checkerboard 3 is at the bottom of the scarf, and Triangle Block 6 is above it. With RS facing, larger needles, dark olive, and working in the row 13 rows below the blue-purple stripe that is now above Triangle Block 6, pick up and knit the last 20 sts of the row. Work 13 rows St st, beg and ending with a WS row. Join light green.

CHECKERBOARD FACING

Row 1: (RS) K3 dark olive, *k2 light green, k2 dark olive; rep from * to last 5 sts, k2 light green, k3 dark olive.

Row 2: P3 dark olive, *p2 light green, p2 dark olive; rep from * to last 5 sts, p2 light green, p3 dark olive.

Row 3: K3 light green, *k2 dark olive, k2 light green; rep from * to last 5 sts, k2 dark olive, k3 light green.

Nine Patch

	color A*
✕	color B*
●	blue-purple
☐	light green
—	orange
◢	burgundy

*See text for color information

Row 4: P3 light green *p2 dark olive, p2 light green; rep from * to last 5 sts, p2 dark olive, p3 light green.

Rows 5 and 6: Rep Rows 1 and 2.

Change to orange and knit 1 RS row, then knit 1 WS row for turning ridge. Work 4 rows St st. BO all sts. With orange, work a line of horizontal running stitches in the orange row just below the turning ridge. With orange, work a line of backstitches on every st in the last row of dark olive before the checkerboard facing. Fold facing along turning ridge and slip-stitch to WS of pocket. Sew inner vertical edge of pocket to scarf. Weave in loose ends. Leave the rem pocket side unattached for now; it will be joined to the layer below when the edging is applied.

FILLER CORD COVERING

The filler cord covering is worked in short, two-color knitted sections that are assembled into a long piece that is then stitched around the outside of the cord. The cord covering shown was worked on size 6 (4-mm) needles with four of the yarn's six plies, and required fourteen covering units, and one partial unit. You may also use size 7 (4.5-mm) needles and the entire strand of yarn as it comes from the ball, but you may need a different number of covering sections; cut the filler cord to the length of your scarf first, and work enough units to cover the cord. Each section is worked with blue-purple (MC), color A, and color B (see below for combinations used in the scarf shown). Work 1 covering unit in each of the foll color combinations (given as A/B); all use blue-purple for the MC: light green/orange, light green/dark olive, dark olive/violet, violet/orange, violet/burgundy, burgundy/orange. Work 2 covering units in each of the foll color combinations with blue-purple as MC: light green/violet, light green/burgundy, dark olive/orange, dark olive/burgundy. **_Covering unit:_** With blue-purple and 4 plies if using smaller dpn, and all 6 plies if using larger dpn, CO 37 sts. All slipped sts are slipped as if to purl.

Row 1: (RS) [Sl 1 st with yarn in back (wyib), k1 A] 9 times, [sl 1 wyib, k1 B] 9 times, end sl 1 wyib.

Row 2: Slide sts back to beg of needle and work another RS row as foll: *K1 MC, sl 1 wyib; rep from * to last st, end k1 MC. Turn work.

Row 3: (WS) [Sl 1 with yarn in front (wyif), p1 B] 9 times, [sl 1 wyif, p1 A] 9 times, end sl 1 wyif.

Row 4: Slide sts back to beg of needle and work another WS row as foll: *P1 MC, sl 1 wyif; rep from * to last st, end p1 MC.

Rep Rows 1–4 once more, then work Rows 1 and 2 once—10 rows completed that look like vertical stripes, each 5 sts high. With blue-purple, BO all sts.

If using four plies of yarn and smaller dpn, make a partial unit by CO 21 sts with blue-purple, and working as for full unit using violet throughout (no third color). Cut the filler cord to the length of the scarf. Lay the covering units side-by-side in an arrangement you find pleasing; do not let the same color combination appear next to itself. With yarn threaded on a tapestry needle, sew the units tog to make a single wide piece of knitting with vertical stripes. Wrap the covering around the filler cord and sew the CO and BO edges tog to enclose the cord, stretching or easing the covering to fit. Sew the ends shut. Sew the covered cord to the long edge of the scarf that has pockets, sewing through all layers at the pocket edges to finish the pockets.

FINISHING

Fold the 8-row St st sections at each end of the scarf in half to the RS with their purl sides facing out, and slip-stitch in place. On the rem long side, using crochet hook and orange, work 2 rows of slip-stitch crochet (see Glossary). Weave in loose ends and block.

LINING

Prepare a lining piece 1" (2.5 cm) wider and 1" (2.5 cm) longer than the scarf; you may have to piece the lining together, depending on how wide your material is. Fold under ½" (1.3 cm) all the way around and press. Sew lining to back of scarf with sewing needle and thread.

Tiny beads, subtle embroidery, and a striped corded edging add interesting detail to this color-block scarf.

FLORAL TRELLIS SCARF
ANN BUDD

Ann Budd has chosen a plush, cotton chenille yarn in rich shades of burgundy and red for this somewhat dressy, somewhat funky crocheted scarf. The base is a simple trellis grid crocheted in chain stitches. The roses are strips of knitted "ruffles" that are curled into flower shapes and sewn in place with sewing thread. Says Ann, "Think of this scarf as a cross between a scarf, a shawl, and a boa."

TRELLIS BASE

FIRST HALF

With MC and crochet hook (see Glossary for crochet instructions), loosely ch 301 sts. Turn.

Row 1: 1 sc into 14th st of chain, *ch 7, skip 6 sts, 1 sc into next (7th) st; rep from *, ending 1 sc in last st of chain—42 trellis holes. Turn.

Row 2: Ch 1, work 1 sl st in each of the first 4 sts of ch-7 loop of previous row, *ch 7, 1 sc into 4th st of next ch-7 loop of previous row; rep from *, ending with 1 sc—41 holes. Turn.

Row 3: Ch 1, work 1 sl st in each of the first 4 sts of ch-7 of previous row, *ch 7, 1 sc into 4th st of next ch-7 loop of previous row; rep from *, ending with 1 sc—40 holes. Turn.

Row 4: Rep Row 2—39 holes.

Row 5: Rep Row 2, but do not turn—38 holes.

EDGING

Ch 1, turn, work 1 sl st in each of the first 4 sts of ch-7 loop of previous row, *ch 4, 1 sc in 4th st of next ch-7 loop of previous row; rep from * to last ch-7 loop—37 holes. Fasten off.

SECOND HALF

Turn first half around so that original ch 301 is facing (now looks like a scalloped edge), join MC to center of hole on right edge, and cont as foll:

Row 1: *Ch 7, 1 sc into 7th st of chain; rep from *, ending 1 sc in last ch-7 loop, ch 1, turn—41 holes.

Row 2: Work 1 sl st in each of the first 4 sts of ch-7 loop of previous row, * ch 7, 1 sc into 4th st of next ch-7 loop of previous row; rep from *, ending with 1 sc—40 holes. Turn.

FINISHED SIZE

Trellis base measures about 7" (18 cm) wide and 50" (127 cm) long; roses measure about 2¾" (7 cm) in diameter.

YARN

Crystal Palace Cotton Chenille (100% cotton; 98 yd [89 m]/50 g): #9121 dark burgundy (MC), 2 skeins; #4519 mauve, #4021 red, #8166 tomato red, and #4212 dark grape, 1 skein each.

NEEDLES

Size 8 (5 mm). Adjust needle size if necessary to obtain the correct gauge.

NOTIONS

Size H/8 (5-mm) crochet hook; tapestry needle; safety pins (optional); sewing thread to match MC; sewing needle.

GAUGE

Not critical for this project.

Row 3: Rep Row 2—39 holes.
Row 4: Rep Row 2, but do not turn—38 holes.

EDGING

Ch 1, turn, work 1 sl st in each of the first 4 sts of ch-7 loop of previous row, *ch 4, 1 sc in 4th st of next ch-7 loop of previous row; rep from * to last ch-7 loop—37 holes. Fasten off.

ROSES

Make 12 knitted ruffles—2 MC, 4 mauve, 2 red, 2 tomato red, and 2 dark grape—as foll:
With size 8 needles, CO 6 sts.
Rows 1, 3, 5, and 7: Purl.
Row 2: *K1f&b; rep from *—12 sts.
Row 4: Rep Row 2—24 sts.
Row 6: Rep Row 2—48 sts.
Row 8: Rep Row 2—96 sts.
With WS facing, BO all sts knitwise. Break yarn, leaving an 8" (20.5-cm) tail. Spiral ruffle into a rose shape, thread tail on a tapestry needle, and tack into position.

FINISHING

Weave in loose ends. Pin six roses to each end of trellis base in a pleasing arrangement as shown in photograph, extending roses about one-third of the way from each end, and leaving the middle one-third of scarf without roses. With sewing thread and needle, sew roses in place.

BEADS OF EARTH
JANE DAVIS

Jane Davis likes to pair the soft, fluid feel of knitted fabric with the crisp texture of beads. In this warm, earth-toned scarf, she uses a beading technique that was popular for making knitted purses and bags in the early 1900s. The beads are strung onto the yarn before knitting and slid into place between stitches as needed. It's a simple way to work with beads, yet the gentle arcs formed by the beaded sections make an impressive finish to an otherwise plain scarf. The close color match of beads and yarn is subtle and sophisticated. Choose shinier beads and a bright yarn for a stand-out version.

STITCH GUIDE

B#: Slide the specified number of beads up close to the right needle, then work the next stitch so the beads are sitting on the strand of yarn between the stitch before and the stitch after the B# instruction.

NOTES

❖ When working with beads and yarn, consider the compatibility of the yarn and beads. The beads need to have holes large enough to accommodate the yarn, and the yarn needs to be strong enough to allow the beads to slide back and forth without breaking. The yarn should also be smooth enough that the beads don't get hung up on slubs or other textured spots. It's a good idea to try the beads and yarn together in a test swatch to see if you like how they look and act together.

❖ To keep the yarn threaded with beads from tangling as you work, place the beaded yarn in a bowl or basket and let the part of the yarn with beads on it coil loosely in the container. You can slide the beads up to the needle for inserting them into the work, or push them back down the yarn, away from the needle, to give you enough unbeaded yarn for knitting.

❖ Slide about 4" (10 cm) to 6" (15 cm) of beads along the yarn at one time to avoid wear and tear on the yarn.

❖ The number in parentheses at the beginning of each row is the number of beads needed for that row. If you slide that number of beads up to your working area and have about 24" (61 cm) of unbeaded yarn free in front of the rest of the beads, you will have enough yarn to knit the row and you will be able to double check that you knit the row accurately, since you'd pre-counted the number of beads needed for the row just worked.

FINISHED SIZE
6" (15 cm) wide with edges unrolled, and 48" (122 cm) long.

YARN
Cascade Yarns pima Silk (85% pima cotton, 15% silk; 109 yd [100 m]/50 g): #5224 taupe, 6 skeins.

NEEDLES
Size 7 (4.5 mm). Adjust needle size if necessary to obtain the correct gauge.

NOTIONS
45 grams of size 6 matte brown seed beads (about 714 beads); bead stringing needle; stitch holders; tapestry needle.

GAUGE
20 sts and 24 rows = 4" (10 cm) in St st.

SCARF HALF

String 357 beads onto one ball of yarn.

Preparation Row: (42 beads) CO 3 sts, slide 6 beads up to the needle, [CO 4 sts, slide 6 beads up to the needle] 6 times, CO 3 sts—30 sts CO; 7 groups of 6 beads each.

Row 1: (35 beads) K3, B5 (see Stitch Guide), [k4, B5] 6 times, k3.

Row 2: (33 beads) P3, B4, [p4, B5] 5 times, p4, B4, p3.

Row 3: (31 beads) K3, B4, k4, B4, [k4, B5] 3 times, [k4, B4] 2 times, k3.

Row 4: (27 beads) P3, B3, [p4, B4] 2 times, p4, B5, [p4, B4] 2 times, p4, B3, p3.

Row 5: (26 beads) K3, B3, [k4, B4] 5 times, k4, B3, k3.

Row 6: (22 beads) P3, B2, p4, B3, [p4, B4] 3 times, p4, B3, p4, B2, p3.

Row 7: (22 beads) K3, B2, k4, B3, [k4, B4] 3 times, k4, B3, k4, B2, k3.

Row 8: (18 beads) P3, B1, [p4, B3] 2 times, p4, B4, [p4, B3] 2 times, p4, B1, p3.

Row 9: (16 beads) K3, B1, k4, B2, k4, B3, k4, B4, k4, B3, k4, B2, k4, B1, k3.

Row 10: (15 beads) P3, B1, p4, B2, [p4, B3] 3 times, p4, B2, p4, B1, p3.

Row 11: (15 beads) K3, B1, k4, B2, [k4, B3] 3 times, k4, B2, k4, B1, k3.

Row 12: (9 beads) P7, B1, p4, B2, p4, B3, p4, B2, p4, B1, p7.

Row 13: (9 beads) K7, B1, k4, B2, k4, B3, k4, B2, k4, B1, k7.

Row 14: (9 beads) Rep Row 12.

Row 15: (8 beads) K7, B1, [k4, B2] 3 times, k4, B1, k7.

Row 16: (4 beads) P11, B1, p4, B2, p4, B1, p11.

Row 17: (4 beads) K11, B1, k4, B2, k4, B1, k11.

Rows 18 and 19: (4 beads each) Rep Rows 16 and 17.

Row 20: (1 bead) P15, B1, p15.

Row 21: (1 bead) K15, B1, k15.

Rows 22 and 23: (1 bead each) Rep Rows 20 and 21.

Work even in St st until piece measures 24" (61 cm) from beg. Place sts on a holder. Make a second scarf half same as the first.

FINISHING

With yarn threaded on a tapestry needle and using the Kitchener st (see Glossary), graft live sts of two halves tog. Weave in loose ends. Steam-press to block.

designNOTEBOOK

IDEAS FOR INVENTING YOUR OWN SCARF

An idea for a scarf design can come from anywhere, an irresistible yarn, a stitch pattern that appeals to you, a crocheted border you'd like to try, or perhaps a collection of beads that would make a wonderful fringe. Starting a project without a pattern, however, even a simple scarf, might cause you to hesitate, whether you're a new or experienced knitter. Where to begin? This chapter provides you with a myriad of knitting possibilities for inventing your own scarf, and some basic guidelines for putting yarn to needles. Even if your knitting skills are limited to the knit stitch, you'll find several ways to make even the basic garter stitch scarf interesting and individual. Whatever your skill level or experience, there's no better way to develop confidence in your craft than to design and knit your own scarf.

**BACKYARD LEAVES | ANNIE MODESITT

GETTING STARTED
CHOOSING YARN

Finding a great yarn in an appealing color and sumptuous fiber is a good jumping off place for a first scarf. Make sure that the yarn you choose is soft and will be comfortable around the neck. Yarns today come in many fibers and blends of fibers. Even certain wools are smooth and soft enough to make luscious scarves. How much yarn you'll need for a scarf will depend on the dimensions of the scarf you'd like to make and how much area each ball or skein of yarn will make when knitted up. Once you've knitted up your first ball or skein of yarn, you'll know how many inches of scarf each ball will yield.

GARTER-STITCH IDEAS
TOP TO BOTTOM:
Garter-stitch worked on the diagonal, garter-stitch squares knitted in different directions, garter-stitch on big needles.

THE NOT-SO-BASIC GARTER-STITCH SCARF

A garter-stitch scarf is the simplest scarf to make. It lies flat, it's fairly mindless to knit, and given the yarn you use, a garter-stitch scarf can look comfortably rustic or downtown flashy. For a beginning knitter, making a garter-stitch scarf is a good way to become familiar with the movements of knitting and to practice making smooth, even stitches. But even experienced knitters can find ways to make a garter-stitch scarf interesting to knit. You can:

❖ vary a garter-stitch scarf by working it in an unexpected direction—horizontally from end to end, vertically from side to side, or on the diagonal

❖ make a "lace" scarf by working with a fine yarn and a very large needle size

❖ make a striped scarf by using different yarns in different colors, textures, fibers, etc.

❖ work any chevron or scalloped stitch pattern exclusively in garter stitch (basic directions for these are found in the section on stripes)

❖ make a 'pieced' scarf by knitting a small section and picking up stitches along the edges to knit adjoining patches

❖ embellish the ends with pom-poms, beaded fringe, tassels made from a variety of yarns, or add a crocheted border

NEEDLE SIZE

Knitting needles are the workhorses of knitting and few of us think of them as a design tool. For the most part, we play around with needle size only when we're trying to make our stitches match a certain size or gauge. But the size of the needle you use for a given yarn will determine the size of the individual stitches, which in turn will determine the drape and feel of the knitted fabric. A small needle in combination with a heavy yarn will make tight, dense stitches that yield a stiff fabric. But increase the circumference of the needle, and the fabric will loosen up and become soft and pliable. You can use these different effects in designing. If you use large needles consistently with a fingering or lace-weight yarn, the stitches will be open, airy, and lace-like. However, if you alternate several rows worked on large needles with rows worked on small needles, you can create a subtle striped texture that waves in and out slightly along the edges.

Experiment with
scarf possibilities
by working the
same stitch pattern
in a variety of
different yarns.

CHOOSING A STITCH PATTERN

After you've found a yarn you like, think about what kind of look you want your scarf to have, what kind of stitch or color pattern will show your yarn to advantage. Do you want a scarf that's textured or smooth? Cabled or ribbed? Lacey and open? Striped or patterned?

Scarves can be worked in any of the hundreds of knitted stitch patterns collected in stitch encyclopedias. (See page 148 for a list of some of these books.) Stitch patterns—knit-and-purl variations, ribs, cables, lace, and slip stitches—yield many different textures and looks, but they also determine another characteristic of your scarf, whether it lies flat or curls into a tube.

A scarf worked in **stockinette stitch** or any pattern that has more knitted stitches than purls on a given side (stockinette-stitch has *only* knit stitches on one side, and *only* purl stitches on the other) will roll toward the purl side along its length. You can take advantage of the curling tendency of knitted fabric to make a narrow scarf that doesn't feel skimpy. Simply work a stockinette-stitch scarf several inches wider than you'd like it to be. It will curl into a tube yielding a narrow scarf with the body of several layers of fabric. Fine yarns, especially silky ones, lend themselves well to this kind of graceful tube-like scarf.

In contrast, a scarf worked in a pattern with a balanced number of knit and purl stitches on the same side of the fabric, such as **garter stitch, seed stitch**, or some type of **ribbed pattern**, will resist curling. And many of these patterns are reversible. The plaid knit-and-purl pattern used by Fiona Ellis in her Campus Scarf (page 26) is a good example of a balanced stitch pattern that lies flat and reads the same from either side.

KNIT-AND-PURL STITCH PATTERNS

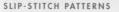

SLIP-STITCH PATTERNS

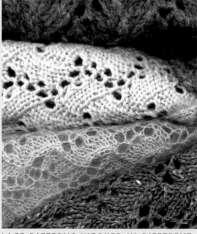

LACE PATTERNS WORKED IN DIFFERENT YARNS

CAMPUS SCARF | FIONA ELLIS   **MISTY GARDEN** | JO SHARP

Some **slip-stitch patterns,** where certain stitches are slipped from the left-hand needle to the right without being worked, will also lie flat. Slip-stitch patterns can be worked in a solid color for a textured scarf, but they can also be worked in changing colors. Many slip-stitch patterns have a woven look, and certain ones called "mosaics" have a distinctive, geometric appearance.

Lace stitches can be beautiful in scarves. Some lace patterns are so open and airy they look like cobwebs. Others are "lace" by virtue of an eyelet here and there. Lace patterns vary in their tendency to curl; those that show some purl stitches on the right side are less likely to roll. While nothing is more beautiful than a traditional scarf in lace-weight mohair, lace stitches needn't be limited to fine yarns and small needles. Part of the fun of designing a lace scarf is playing with the unexpected. Annie Modesitt has used a worsted-weight Merino in her leaf-and-lace scarf (page 79), and Jo Sharp used a variegated mohair for her scarf, Misty Garden, worked in the timeless Feather and Fan pattern (page 50). Try swatching lace patterns in a variety of yarns. And don't overlook the interesting possibilities of working a lace scarf in a rustic tweed, a nubby silk, a smooth Merino, or an unspun Icelandic wool.

Stitch patterns that balance knit and purl stitches on each side will lie flat.

REVERSIBLE RIBBED CABLE PANEL (WORKED OVER 20 STS)

ROW 1: (RS) [K1, p1] 3 times, pm, [k1, p1] 4 times, pm, [k1, p1] 3 times.

ROWS 2–4: Work in rib as established, slipping markers.

ROW 5: (RS) Work in rib as established to marker, slip marker (sl m), sl 4 sts onto cn and hold in back, [k1, p1] twice, work 4 sts from cn as [k1, p1] twice, sl m, work in rib to end.

ROWS 6–13: Work in rib as established, slipping markers.

ROW 14: (WS) Work in rib as established to marker, sl m, sl 4 sts onto cn and hold in back [k1, p1] twice, work 4 sts from cn as [k1, p1] twice, sl m, work in rib to end.

ROWS 15–18: Work in rib as established, slipping markers.

Repeat Rows 1–18 for pattern.

NOTE: You can work the stitches in between cable panels in stitch patterns other than ribs, e.g. garter stitch, seed stitch, etc.

Cables are a natural design element for knitted scarves. Worked from one end of a scarf to the other, nothing interferes with their fluid intertwining movement. You can work them as isolated panels against a simple background (garter stitch is a good choice because it won't curl on the edges), as an element in an Aran-based design (see Mags Kandis's scarf, Fair Isle Jazz, page 19), or use them as an allover pattern as Norah Gaughan and Shirley Paden have (pages 14 and 40). If you work cables in a ribbed pattern and alternate the rows on which you turn the cables, your scarf will be reversible (see Lisa Daniels's scarf, page 76).

If you'd like your scarf to lay flat but don't want to use a non-curling stitch, there are several ways to thwart the rolling tendency in knitted fabric. You can knit a scarf in the round to make a closed tube, which will make a substantial, cozy scarf if worked in a fingering or sportweight yarn (heavier yarns will be too thick). But be aware that a scarf worked double will take twice as long to knit because it is essentially two scarves back to back. Another option is to work an inch or so of a non-curling stitch pattern, such as garter or seed stitch, along the edges of the scarf. A non-curling border won't eliminate the roll completely, but it will discourage it. You can also line your scarf to prevent it from curling in. Use a patterned fabric (see Paula Jenne's scarf, page 112) to add spark, or a subtle fabric that blends with the overall color of your design (see Nicky Epstein's Dragon Scarf, page 36). If you want to stick with knitting, work a knitted lining as Mags Kandis did for the Fair Isle portions of her scarf (page 19).

NASTY DOG DRAGON | NICKY EPSTEIN

HERE AND THERE CABLES | NORAH GAUGHAN

LADY ELEANOR ENTRELAC |
KATHLEEN POWER JOHNSON

COLOR ON COLOR | KATHRYN ALEXANDER

KNITTING IN DIFFERENT DIRECTIONS

Most often, scarves are worked by casting on stitches for the width of the scarf and knitting from one narrow end to the other. But they can also be worked from one long edge to the other. (See Kristin Nicholas's scarf on page 12 and Mari Lynn Patrick's crocheted scarf on page 70.) Starting at one long edge and working across to the other is a convenient way to work vertical stripes without having to use a separate bobbin of yarn for each color. A scarf can also be worked on the diagonal, starting with a stitch or two at one corner (see instructions at right). Any surface pattern you use—stripes, stitch patterns, lace, or cables—will change in orientation depending on the direction in which you work your scarf.

Scarves don't have to be worked in a continuous fashion. They can be knitted in sections, each worked in different directions. Kathryn Alexander used intarsia to work a "pieced" center panel, then picked up stitches along the length of the scarf and worked at a right angle to make a colorful striped border (page 57). Kathleen Power Johnson used entrelac, a method of knitting sections that alternate in direction, for her over-sized shawl (page 52). Although it isn't strictly necessary, garter stitch lends itself well to a scarf worked in sections or "pieced" together.

HOW TO KNIT A GARTER-STITCH SCARF ON THE DIAGONAL

To work a garter-stitch scarf on the diagonal, you don't need to determine your gauge or the width or length of your scarf ahead of time. Instead, begin at a corner with just two stitches, and work as described here until your scarf is as long as you'd like, or you run out of yarn. For instructions on how to increase and decrease stitches, see the Glossary.

Cast on 2 sts.

ROW 1: K1, k1f&b in next st (1 st increased)—3 sts.

ROW 2: K2, k1f&b in last s—4 sts. Cont to work in garter stitch, increasing 1 st in the last st of every row until the scarf is as wide as you'd like it. Mark one side as a RS row.

NEXT (RS) ROW: Knit to last 2 sts, ssk.

NEXT ROW: Knit to last st, k1f&b.

Repeat the last 2 rows until the scarf is as long as you'd like it, ending with a WS row.

NEXT ROW (RS): Knit to last 2 sts, ssk.

NEXT ROW: Knit to last 2 sts, ssk.

Repeat the last 2 rows until 2 sts remain. Bind off.

NOTE: These instructions work only for stitch patterns, like garter stitch, in which the number of stitches per inch equals the number of rows per inch. To work a scarf on the diagonal in another stitch pattern, you'll need to adjust the rate of increases and decreases to make an even rectangle. There isn't a standard formula for this because the rate depends on your gauge, but if you follow the instructions above and tinker with the number of rows to work between increases and decreases, you'll be able to work any stitch on the diagonal.

MAKE A STRIPED SCARF

FINISHED SIZE
About 10" (25 cm) wide and 78" (198 cm) long, or desired length.

YARN
Classic Elite Montera (50% llama, 50% wool; 127 yd [115 m]/100 g): Any colors, 4 skeins.

NEEDLES
Size 9 (5.5 mm).

GAUGE
20 sts and 20 rows = 4" in rib pattern when slightly stretched and blocked.

SCARF
Cast on 51 stitches.

ROW 1: Sl 1 kwise, *k1, p1; rep from *, end k2.

ROW 2: Sl 1 pwise, * p1, k1; rep from *, end p2.

Repeat Rows 1 and 2, changing colors for stripe pattern, until scarf measures 78" or desired length.

POSSIBLE STRIPE PATTERN (4 COLORS):

COLOR #1: 8 rows.
COLOR #2: 4 rows.
COLOR #3: 2 rows.
COLOR #4: 2 rows.

Repeat 16-row sequence for stripe pattern.

COLORWORK
STRIPES

Stripes are a simple way to get lots of color into a scarf. They can be soothingly predictable in a repeating pattern, or eye-catching in a random, unexpected arrangement. They can be worked in two, three, or dozens of colors. They can each have the same width or they can vary, by a lot or a little. Stripes can be thick—two inches, four inches, six inches or more—or as narrow as one knitted row. You can combine thick stripes with thin stripes.

Knitting stripes is a good way to learn how colors work together and how varying the proportion of one color to another contributes to the overall feel of a project. Stripes in similar colors, say, reds, umbers, and oranges, will blend together somewhat and create a soft transition between colors. Stripes in contrasting colors, such as red, aqua, yellow, or in colors of different values (light and dark), will make a bold, vibrant scarf.

The character of the yarn used in a stripe pattern will also affect the way the stripes read. In clear solid colors, stripes will look crisp. Stripes worked in heather or tweed yarns will be softer and more muted, especially if the colors are close in hue. A stripe pattern that uses a variety of yarn types—a smooth yarn, a tweedy yarn, a bouclé, a chenille—will have the feel of folk art, art that makes aesthetic use of what's at hand.

You can turn a simple color-stripe pattern into a complex design by changing stitch patterns in conjunction with color changes, or in counterpoint to them. And you can create a mismatched stripe pattern by knitting several narrow bands in different striped patterns, and then joining them together along their lengths.

Stripes can run horizontally—perpendicular to the length of the scarf, or vertically—parallel to the length of the scarf, or diagonally—starting from one lower corner to the opposite upper corner. Stripes can zigzag or form wavy patterns when worked in a chevron or scalloped stitch pattern (see Debblie Bliss's ZigZag Stripes scarf on page 33). Sample chevron and scalloped patterns are provided on page 136.

Although most of us think of colors when we think of stripes, stripes can also be created with textures. For example, alternating bands of reverse stockinette stitch (the "wrong" side of stockinette stitch) and stockinette stitch will create pronounced horizontal ridges or welts from side to side. Deep ribs make for vertical "stripes." If you alternate a section of ribs with a section of welts, a wavy pattern will form. The ribbed sections will draw in and the welt sections will spread out.

ZIGZAG STRIPES | DEBBIE BLISS   **ROSEBUD SCARF** | SASHA KAGAN

COLORWORK STITCHES

Next to **stripes,** the simplest way to add color is to work **slip-stitch patterns** that alternate colors every two rows. The beauty of slip-stitch patterns is that only one color is used in a row, just as in working stripes. But the slipped stitches create a color pattern quite unlike a plain stripe.

More complicated to work, and more varied in their appearance, are **Fair Isle** and **intarsia** patterns. Fair Isle patterns, generally speaking, are small motifs that repeat across a row. The ends of Mags Kandis's scarf on page 19 are worked in a variety of Fair Isle patterns. Intarsia patterns, in contrast, consist of larger areas of colorwork and frequently form "pictures," such as the dragon in Nicky Epstein's scarf (page 36) and the flowers on Sasha Kagan's (page 46).

Fair Isle and intarsia patterns have definite right and wrong sides. However, you can make the "wrong" side of a Fair Isle pattern as attractive as the "right" if you are consistent in how you manipulate the yarn at color changes. If you always pick up the background color from underneath the pattern color, or vice-versa, the wrong side, though different from the right, will "read" as a pattern, with the floats (strands) forming the pattern.

The wrong side of intarsia patterns, if worked neatly, can also be interesting. For the flower design in her scarf, Sasha Kagan carried the background color across the wrong side of the motif as she worked, weaving it in every other stitch. The result is a stippled version of the right-side motif. The wrong side of the flower looks like a woven version of the right side.

If you want to avoid having the wrong side of a scarf exposed, work it in a tube (either by knitting the piece in the round or by folding it in half lengthwise and sewing the two edges together). But keep in mind that doing so will create a scarf that is twice as thick. Use a lightweight yarn to keep the scarf soft and pliable. Another option is to cover the wrong side with a lining, as Paula Jenne (page 112), Nicky Epstein (page 36), and Mags Kandis (page 19) chose to do.

Make a striped scarf more interesting by working it in a chevron pattern or knitting it lengthwise.

CHEVRON PATTERN

To make a scarf in a chevron pattern, cast on a multiple of 12 stitches, plus 3 stitches to balance the pattern, and work as follows:

ROW 1: (RS) K1, ssk, *k9, sl 2 sts individually pwise, k1, p2sso; rep from * to last 12 sts, k9, k2tog, k1.

ROW 2: K1, *p1, k4, (k1, yo, k1) all in next st, k4; rep from * to last 2 sts, p1, k1.

Repeat Rows 1 and 2 for pattern.

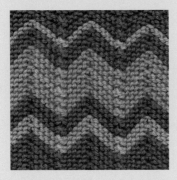

SCALLOPED PATTERN

To make a scarf in a scalloped pattern, cast on a multiple of 13 stitches, plus 2, and work as follows:

ROW 1: (RS) K1, k2tog, k4, yo, *k1, yo, k4, k2tog, ssk, k4, yo; rep from * to last 8 sts, k1, yo, k4, ssk, k1.

ROW 2: Knit.

Repeat Rows 1 and 2 for pattern.

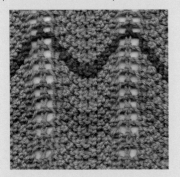

DON'T FORGET THE ENDS

Unless you tuck your scarf inside your coat or jacket, the ends of your scarf are a focal point for design details, such as beading, colorwork, fancy stitch patterns, or interesting fringes, bobbles, pom-poms, tassels, or crocheted edgings. Many stitch patterns—particularly ones in which increases and decreases are worked in vertical columns—form natural decorative borders by causing the cast-on and bound-off edges of the fabric to form scallops or points; see patterns at left for simple chevron and scalloped patterns. Look for other examples in stitch dictionaries listed on page 148.

Stitch patterns designed specifically as borders can vary from a few rows deep to several inches and can be worked vertically or horizontally. For a border worked vertically, the cast-on edge forms the tail end of the scarf. To make a scarf with symmetrical ends, cast on and work the border pattern; then continue knitting in a simple stitch pattern until the scarf measures half the desired length. Place the stitches on a holder. Cast on and work a second piece identical to the first and graft the scarf pieces together at the center back neck. (Instructions for grafting are given in the Glossary.)

For borders that are worked horizontally (side to side) the cast-on edge forms the side edge (selvedge) of the scarf. To use a horizontal border, cast on the number of stitches given in the border pattern and work the pattern for the desired *width* of the scarf, then bind off. Pick up stitches along the straight side edge (top) of one of the border pieces (usually about 3 stitches to every 4 rows of the border) and continue in a simple stitch pattern to the center back. Make a second piece the same as the first and graft the two together at the center back neck.

SCARF ENDS
TOP TO BOTTOM:
scalloped border made from Bear Track pattern, Lacey border worked horizontally, Fringed end.

ENE'S SCARF | NANCY BUSH   **TURTLENECK SHRUG** | TEVA DURHAM

SHAPES AND SIZES

A scarf doesn't have to be a long rectangle. It can be triangular, worked from the wide base and shaped with decreases along the outer edges to the point, or it can be worked from the pointed end and increased to the base. Nancy Bush's Triangular scarf, Ene's scarf, (page 29) is worked from the outside edges and shaped with decreases along the outer edges as well as along the center axis.

Sally Melville's scarf (page 86) is shaped in the opposite direction, from the point to the wide base. The "points" at the outer edges of the base are extended to form ties that wrap around the neck.

A stole or shawl is a scarf on a larger scale, ample enough to wrap comfortably around the contour of the shoulders and upper torso. It can be an exaggerated rectangle, a triangle, or an innovative combination of shapes. Catherine Lowe created a luxurious wrap by working a series of four connecting triangles that form a large square (page 88).

A cowl is essentially a scarf without ends, a tube that can slip on and off like a detachable collar or turtleneck. Cowls lack the romantic and dramatic possibilities of a scarf whose ends can be thrown around the neck or flutter in the breeze. But cowls are cozy and convenient, and they fit neatly into a pocket when not in use. Teva Durham has taken the neck cowl a step further by adding sleeves to it, in her Turtleneck Shrug (page 83).

A cowl that forms a tube wide enough to fit over the shoulders can function like a wrap. It hugs your shoulders, a little like swaddling, and though it may limit arm movement to some extent, unlike shawls and stoles, you don't need to use your hands to keep it from sliding off.

A scarf doesn't have to be a long rectangle. A triangular scarf or scarf-cum-shrug will keep your shoulders warm.

Simple or complex, plain or ruffled, scarves are fun to make and wear.

TIME TO BEGIN

Once you've determined the stitch pattern you'd like to use, you'll need to make a sample swatch to make sure your stitch pattern, yarn, and needle size will work together to make a pleasing scarf. Before you cast on, you'll need to choose needles that will work with your yarn to create the effect you want. Yarn labels usually suggest a needle size to use with their yarn, and the suggested size is a good place to start. But don't feel you can't change needles if the resulting fabric doesn't have the loft or drape you'd like. The only way to find out what your scarf will look like is to knit a sample swatch. Cast on about 25 stitches, or a multiple of the stitch pattern you plan to use, and work the pattern until the swatch measures about 4" (10 cm). Take a look at what you've made. Does it feel soft and springy? Do the stitches look neat and tidy? Then you probably have a good yarn-and-needle match. If your sample feels tight and stiff, try again with a larger needle. If your swatch looks loose and sloppy, try a smaller one. Experiment until you're happy with the fabric you're making. (Use your finished sample as a gauge swatch. For more about finding gauge, see the Glossary.)

Next, decide how wide you'd like your scarf to be. If in doubt, measure a scarf that you already own and go from there. Then multiply your gauge (the number of stitches per inch in your swatch) by how wide, in inches, you'd like your scarf to measure.

For example, if you want a scarf that's ten inches wide and your gauge is five stitches in one inch:

10 inches x 5 stitches/inch = 50 stitches to cast on

RUFFLED CAPELET WITH SLEEVES | PAM ALLEN   **MIDWEST MOONLIGHT** | IVY BIGELOW

BLIZZARD | LEIGH RADFORD   **BLUE COLLAR** | TEVA DURHAM

If you plan to use garter or stockinette stitch, you can cast on and start knitting. If you'd like to use a stitch pattern that's built on a repeat of a certain number of stitches, you may need to add or subtract stitches from your total number in order to accommodate the number of stitches in the pattern repeat. Most stitch patterns repeat over a set number of stitches, such as 4, 6, or 8, etc. Some patterns require extra stitches to balance the pattern. For example, if the stitch pattern is a "multiple of 4 stitches plus 2" you'll need to cast on a multiple of 4 stitches—for example, 24, 36, or 48, etc.—then add 2 more stitches to balance the pattern at the end of the row. Therefore, you would cast on 26, 38, or 50 stitches for the example above. Then knit until your scarf is as long as you'd like it.

If you've chosen a stitch pattern that has an identifiable top and bottom, in order to make a scarf with two identical ends, you'll need to work your scarf in two pieces—from tail end to the center back—then graft the pieces together. For how to graft knitted pieces together, see the Glossary.

Before casting on, decide if you want to add a border of garter stitch, seed stitch or another stable, non-rolling stitch along the outer edges. If you'd like a 3-stitch border along the edges of your scarf, add 6 more stitches to your cast-on number—3 for each side. Begin your scarf by working several rows of the border stitch across all the stitches. When you're ready to start the pattern stitch, work the first 3 stitches in the border pattern (place a marker on your needle at this point, if it will help you to remember to work the border stitches independently of the pattern stitch), work the pattern stitch to the last 3 stitches, place another marker, and work the last 3 stitches in the border pattern. End the scarf by working several rows of the border stitch across all the stitches before binding off.

Think of scarves in terms of scale, think large and make an enveloping shawl; think small and make a silky collar.

GLOSSARY OF TERMS AND TECHNIQUES

BIND-OFFS
STANDARD BIND-OFF
Slip 1 stitch, *knit 1 stitch, insert the left needle tip into the first stitch on the right needle (Figure 1), pass this stitch over the second stitch (Figure 2), and off the needle—1 stitch remains on the right needle and 1 stitch has been bound off (Figure 3). Repeat from *.

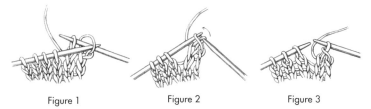

Figure 1   Figure 2   Figure 3

THREE-NEEDLE BIND-OFF
Place the stitches to be joined onto two separate needles. Hold the needles so that the right sides of the knitting face together. Insert a third needle into the first stitch on each of the other two needles and knit them together as one stitch (Figures 1 & 2), *knit the next stitch on each needle together in the same way, then pass the first stitch over the second (Figure 3). Repeat from * until one stitch remains on the third needle. Cut yarn and pull the tail through the last stitch.

Figure 1   Figure 2   Figure 3

BLOCKING
There are various ways to block a knitted scarf, depending on the yarn fiber, the stitch pattern, and the amount of time you have.

Unless the label on the yarn tells you otherwise, most yarns will benefit from a light steaming. Spread out a couple of beach towels on a mattress, then lay the scarf on top of them. Pin out the corners if necessary and straighten the edges. Hold an iron about an inch above the knitted surface and let the steam penetrate it. Move the iron slowly above the scarf. When you're finished, let the scarf dry thoroughly.

Alternatively, you can wet the scarf by placing it in a sink of cool water. When the scarf is saturated, let the water out of the sink and gently squeeze (but don't wring) out the excess moisture. Spread the scarf out on an open beach towel and roll up the towel loosely from the short end. Press a little on the towel to absorb a bit more moisture. Unroll the towel and lay the scarf out on a dry beach towel, straightening it, molding any cables with your fingers, and evening it out where needed. Pin it in place, if necessary. Let dry.

CABLES
Cables are made when stitches cross over each other, or twist, within a row of knitting. In effect, small groups of stitches change places with each other. You will need a cable needle (a short knitting needle with a point at each end). To make a cable, slip the designated number of stitches (usually 2 or 3) onto a cable needle, hold the cable needle in front of the work for a left-leaning twist (Figure 1) or in back of the work for a right-leaning twist (Figure 2), knit the specified number of stitches from the left needle (usually the same number of stitches that were placed on the cable needle), then work the stitches from the cable needle in the order in which they were placed on the needle (Figure 3).

Figure 1   Figure 2   Figure 3

CAST-ONS

CONTINENTAL (LONG-TAIL) CAST-ON

Leaving a long tail (about ½ to 1" [1.3 to 2.5 cm] for each stitch to be cast on), make a slipknot and place on the right needle. Place thumb and index finger between the yarn ends so that the working yarn is around your index finger and the tail end is around your thumb. Secure the ends with your other fingers and hold palm upward to make a V of yarn (Figure 1).

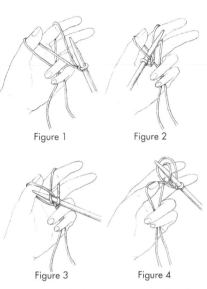

Figure 1   Figure 2

Figure 3   Figure 4

*Bring the needle up through the loop on your thumb (Figure 2), grab the first strand around your index finger with the needle, and go back down through the loop on your thumb (Figure 3), drop the loop off your thumb and, placing your thumb back in the V configuration, tighten the resulting stitch on the needle (Figure 4). Repeat from * for the desired number of stitches.

BACKWARD LOOP CAST-ON

*Loop the working yarn and place it on the needle backward so that it doesn't unwind. Repeat from * for the desired number of stitches.

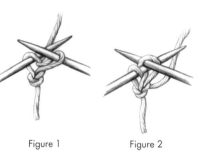

CABLE CAST-ON

Figure 1   Figure 2   Figure 3

Begin with a slipknot and one knitted cast-on stitch if there are no established stitches. Insert the right needle between the first two stitches on the left needle (Figure 1). Wrap the yarn as if to knit. Draw the yarn through to complete the stitch (Figure 2) and slip this new stitch onto the left needle (Figure 3).

KNITTED CAST-ON

Place a slipknot on the left needle if there are no established stitches. *With the right needle, knit into the first stitch (or slipknot) on the left needle (Figure 1) and place the new stitch onto the left needle (Figure 2). Repeat from *, always knitting into the last stitch made.

Figure 1   Figure 2

CHARTS

Charts are visual representations of the knitted fabric viewed from the right side. Charts are plotted on graph paper so that one square represents one stitch and one horizontal row represents one row of knitting. The symbols or colors in the squares indicate how to work each stitch. For colorwork charts, the colors represent yarn colors; for texture work, the symbols represent stitch manipulations. Unless otherwise specified, charts are read from the bottom to the top, and from right to left for right-side rows, from left to right for wrong-side rows. When you're knitting in the round (so that the right side of the knitting is always facing out), all rows are read from right to left.

CROCHET

CROCHET CHAIN (CH)

Make a slipknot and place on crochet hook. *Yarn over hook and draw it through the loop of the slipknot. Repeat from * for desired length. To fasten off, cut the yarn and draw the tail through the last loop formed.

DOUBLE CROCHET (DC)

Yarn over hook, insert the hook into a stitch, yarn over the hook and draw up a loop (three loops on the hook), yarn over the hook (Figure 1) and draw it through two loops, yarn over the hook and draw it through the remaining two loops (Figure 2).

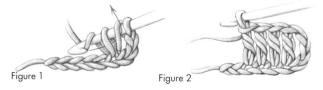

Figure 1   Figure 2

HALF-DOUBLE CROCHET (HDC)

Yarn over hook, insert the hook into a stitch, yarn over the hook and draw up a loop (three loops on the hook), yarn over hook (Figure 1) and draw it through all the loops on the hook (Figure 2).

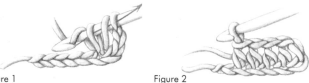

Figure 1   Figure 2

REVERSE SINGLE CROCHET (REV SC)

Working from left to right, insert the crochet hook into a knit edge stitch, draw up a loop, bring the yarn over the hook, and draw this loop through the first one. *Insert the hook into the next stitch to the right (Figure 1), draw up a loop, bring the yarn over the hook again (Figure 2), and draw this loop through both loops on the hook (Figure 3). Repeat from *.

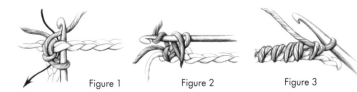

Figure 1   Figure 2   Figure 3

SINGLE CROCHET (SC)

Insert the hook into a stitch, yarn over the hook and draw up a loop, yarn over the hook again (Figure 1), and draw it through both loops on the hook (Figure 2). Repeat from *.

Figure 1   Figure 2

SLIP-STITCH CROCHET (SL ST)

Insert the crochet hook into a stitch, yarn over the hook and draw the loop through the stitch and the loop on the hook.

DECREASES

K2TOG

Knit two stitches together as if they were a single stitch—two stitches are reduced to one.

P2TOG

Purl two stitches together as if they were a single stitch—two stitches are reduced to one.

SSK

Slip two stitches individually knitwise (Figure 1). Insert the tip of the left needle into the front of these two slipped stitches and use the right needle

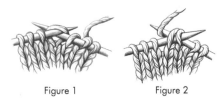

Figure 1   Figure 2

to knit them together through their back loops (Figure 2). (Some knitters like to slip the second stitch purlwise to make a more prominent decrease line.)

SSP

Holding the yarn in front, slip two stitches knitwise one at a time onto the right needle (Figure 1). Slip them back onto the left needle and purl the two stitches together through their back loops (Figure 2).

Figure 1   Figure 2

EMBROIDERY
DUPLICATE STITCH

Bring the threaded needle to the front in the center of a knitted stitch. Following the path of the stitch, bring the needle behind the top of the loop and back through the hole at the

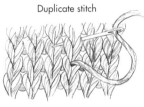

Duplicate stitch

base. Bring the needle up at the base of the next stitch to be covered. Keep the tension of the yarn constant, but not too tight, so that the underlying stitches will be covered but not distorted.

GAUGE

Gauge is an indispensable part of any knitting pattern. Matching gauge is crucial when you're making a sweater with parts that need to fit together and when you want to know ahead of time the dimensions of your final project. When you're knitting a scarf, however, it's not imperative to match a particular gauge. There are no pieces to fit together and exact dimensions aren't as crucial as ending with a soft, pliable fabric that looks good and has the drape and feel of something you'd like to wear around your neck. A scarf will fit even if it's an inch or two wider or narrower, or shorter or longer, than the one in the picture. If you match gauge, and your scarf swatch feels like a piece of cardboard, get a larger needle and swatch until the piece has drape and flexibility. Conversely, if your scarf fabric is looking loose and floppy, use a smaller needle to tighten up the stitches.

To measure gauge, cast on 30 to 40 stitches using the recommended needle size. Work in the specified pattern stitch until the piece measures at least 4" (10 cm) from the cast-on edge. Remove the swatch from the needles or bind off the stitches loosely. Lay the swatch on a flat surface. Place a ruler over the swatch and, in the space of 4" (10 cm), count the number of stitches across and the number of rows down (including fractions of stitches and rows) Repeat this measurement two or three times on different areas of the swatch to confirm your initial measurement. If you have more stitches and rows than called for in the instructions, your stitches are too small and you should try again with larger needles; if you have fewer stitches or rows, your stitches are too large and you should try again with smaller needles. Repeat the process until you get the gauge you're after.

If you find that your gauge is very different from the one given, or you want to adjust the dimensions of the scarf pattern you've chosen, you can add or subtract from the number of stitches to cast on. However, if your scarf is worked in a repeating pattern, be sure to add or subtract the number of stitches in a repeat.

GRAFTING
KITCHENER STITCH

Place the stitches to be joined onto two separate needles. Hold the needles parallel with the points facing to the right and so that the right sides of the knitting are facing you.

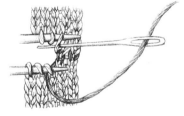

Step 1: Bring the threaded needle through the front stitch as if to purl and leave the stitch on the needle.

Step 2: Bring the threaded needle through the back stitch as if to knit and leave the stitch on the needle.

Step 3: Bring the threaded needle through the same front stitch as if to knit and slip this stitch off the needle, bring the threaded needle through the next front stitch as if to purl and leave this stitch on the needle.

Step 4: Bring the threaded needle through the first back stitch as if to purl (as illustrated), slip that stitch off, bring the needle through the next back stitch as if to knit, leave this stitch on the needle.

Repeat Steps 3 and 4 until no stitches remain on the needles.

INCREASES
RAISED INCREASE (M1)

Unless otherwise indicated, work this increase as M1L.

Left Slant (M1L): With the left needle tip, lift the strand between the needles from front to back (Figure 1). Knit the lifted loop through the back to twist the stitch (Figure 2).

Left Slant

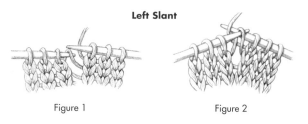

Figure 1   Figure 2

Right Slant (M1R): With the left needle tip, lift the strand between the needles from back to front (Figure 1). Knit the lifted loop through the front to twist the stitch (Figure 2).

Right Slant

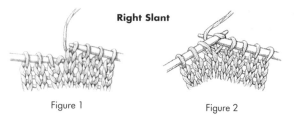

Figure 1   Figure 2

BAR INCREASE (K1F&B)

Knit into a stitch and leave it on the needle (Figure 1), then knit through the back loop of the same stitch (Figure 2), and slip both stitches off the needle.

Figure 1   Figure 2

YARNOVER INCREASE (YO)

Wrap the yarn around the needle from front to back (Figure 1) to create a new loop on the needle.

Yarnover increase

I-CORD
STANDARD I-CORD

With a double-pointed needle, cast on the desired number of stitches (usually 3 to 5). *Without turning the needle, slide the stitches to the other point, pull the yarn around the back, and knit the stitches as usual. Repeat from * for desired length.

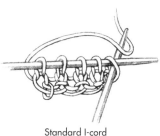

Standard I-cord

ATTACHED I-CORD

As I-cord is knitted, attach it to the garment as follows: With garment RS facing and using a separate ball of yarn and circular needle, pick up the desired number of stitches along the garment edge.

Slide these stitches down the needle so that the first picked-up stitch is near the opposite needle point. With a double-pointed needle, cast on the desired number of I-cord stitches. Knit across the I-cord to the last stitch, then knit the last stitch together with the first picked-up stitch on the garment, and pull the yarn behind the cord. *Knit to the last I-cord stitch, then knit the last I-cord stitch together with the next picked-up stitch and pull the yarn behind the cord. Repeat from * until all picked-up stitches have been used.

KNIT STITCH
CONTINENTAL METHOD

Continental Knit

Hold the working yarn behind the needles and use your right hand to bring the right needle into the first stitch on the left needle from front to back, rotate it counterclockwise (over and behind in a scooping motion) around the taut working yarn, and back out of the stitch, pulling the new stitch through the old as you slide the old stitch off the left needle.

ENGLISH METHOD

English Knit

Hold the working yarn in back of the work and insert the right needle from front to back into the first stitch on the left needle, so that the needle tip extends about an inch (2.5 cm) beyond the stitch. Grasp the right needle with your left thumb and forefinger (without letting go of the left needle), bring the yarn up with your right forefinger, and wrap it around the right needle tip counterclockwise–behind the needle, then to the front between the two needles. Retrieve the right needle with your right hand and use that needle to draw the new stitch through the old as you slide the old stitch off the left needle. Tighten the yarn with your right hand to tension the stitch.

POM-POMS

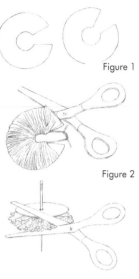

Figure 1

Figure 2

Figure 3

Cut two circles of cardboard, each ½" (1.3 cm) larger than the desired finished pom-pom width. Cut a small circle out of the center and a small wedge out of the side of each circle (Figure 1). Place tie strand between the circles, hold the circles together, and wrap with yarn—the more wraps, the thicker the pom-pom. Cut between the circles and knot the tie strand tightly (Figure 2). Place the pom-pom between two smaller cardboard circles held together with a needle, and trim the edges (Figure 3). This technique comes from *Nicky Epstein's Knitted Embellishments*, Interweave Press, 1999.

PURL STITCH
CONTINENTAL METHOD

Continental Purl

Hold the yarn in front of the work and insert the right needle behind the yarn and down (from front to back) into the first stitch on the left needle. Rotate the right needle around the yarn counterclockwise–over, behind, and around to the front again. Then push the needle to the back, pulling the new stitch through the old and sliding the old stitch off the left needle as you do so.

ENGLISH METHOD

Hold the yarn in front and insert the right needle from back to front into the stitch, so that the tip extends about an inch (2.5 cm) beyond the stitch. Grasp the right needle

English Purl

with your left thumb and forefinger as you use your right forefinger to wrap the yarn around the right needle tip counterclockwise–over and behind the needle, then to the front between the two needles. Move both hands back into their starting position as you use the right needle to draw the new stitch through the old and off the needle. Tighten the stitch with your right hand.

SELVEDGE STITCHES

Scarf edges aren't hidden in seams, and designers frequently use a selvedge stitch or stitches at the outside edges to ensure that the sides of the scarf stay even and neat. Frequently these stitches are worked in a different stitch pattern—say garter stitch—from that used in the body of the scarf. A pattern may call for one or more selvedge stitches and will give instructions for how to knit them.

SHORT ROWS

Short rows are used to add length to a particular area of a row of knitting. To work a short row, work the specified number of stitches to the turning point, slip the next stitch purlwise to the right needle. Bring the yarn to the front (Figure 1). Slip the same stitch back to the left nee-

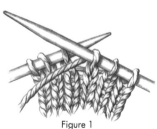

Figure 1

dle (Figure 2). Turn the work and bring the yarn in position for the next stitch, wrapping the slipped stitch as you do so. Hide wraps as follows: *Knit stitch*: On the right side, work to just before the wrapped

stitch, insert the right needle from the front, under the wrap from the bottom up, and then into the wrapped stitch as usual. Knit the stitches together, making sure that the new stitch comes out under the wrap. *Purl stitch*: On the wrong side, work to just before the wrapped stitch. Insert the right

Figure 2

needle from the back, under the wrap from the bottom up, and put it on the left needle. Purl the stitches together.

TASSEL

Cut a piece of cardboard 4" (10 cm) wide by the desired length of the tassel plus 1" (2.5 cm). Wrap the yarn to the desired thickness around the cardboard. Cut a short length of yarn and tie it tightly around one end of the wrapped yarn (Figure 1). Cut yarn loops at the other end. Cut another piece of yarn and wrap tightly around the loops a short distance below the top knot to form the tassel neck. Knot securely, thread the ends onto a tapestry needle, and pull to the center of the tassel (Figure 2). Trim the ends.

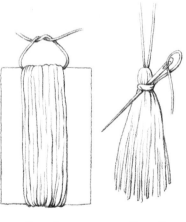

Figure 1   Figure 2

WEAVING IN ENDS

An important step in any knitting pattern is to weave in the loose ends. The ends are the tails of yarn left hanging at the beginning of a project, at the end of the project, and throughout the body of the project wherever a new ball of yarn was joined. All of these ends need to be worked into the knitted fabric to prevent raveling. Depending on the size of your project and the number of colors used, you may have anywhere from two ends (the cast-on tail and the bind-off tail) to dozens of ends to secure. Designers have different ways to do this, but in general, each end is threaded onto a tapestry needle and worked into the wrong side of the fabric. The goal is to make the ends as inconspicuous as possible. When you can, work the ends into seams or at boundaries between stitch patterns where there is already a visual interruption in the knitted fabric. Otherwise, trace the path of a row of stitches (new Figure 1) or work on the diagonal, catching the back side of the stitches (new Figure 2). To reduce bulk, do not weave two ends in the same area. To keep color changes sharp, work the ends into areas of the same color.

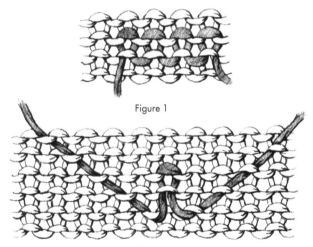

Figure 1

Figure 2

BIBLIOGRAPHY

Harmony Guide, ed. *450 Knitting Stitches—Volume 2*. London: Trafalgar Square, 1998.

Harmony Guide, ed. *440 More Knitting Stitches—Volume 3*. London: Trafalgar Square, 1998.

Harmony Guide, ed. *250 Creative Knitting Stitches—Volume 4*. London, England: Trafalgar Square, 1998.

Harmony Guide, ed. *220 Aran Stitches and Patterns—Volume 5*. London: Trafalgar Square, 1998.

Matthews, Anne. *Vogue Dictionary of Knitting Stitches*. Devon: David & Charles, 1992.

Stanfield, Leslie. *The New Knitting Stitch Library: Over 300 Traditional and Innovative Stitch Patterns*. Asheville, North Carolina: Lark Books, 1999.

Walker, Barbara. *A Treasury of Knitting Patterns*. Pittsville, Wisconsin: Schoolhouse Press, 1998.

_____. *A Second Treasury of Knitting Patterns*. Pittsville, Wisconsin: Schoolhouse Press, 1998.

_____. *Charted Knitting Designs: A Third Treasury of Knitting Patterns*. Pittsville, Wisconsin: Schoolhouse Press, 1998.

BERROCO, INC.
14 Elmdale Rd.
PO Box 367
Uxbridge, MA 01569
www.berroco.com
In Canada: S.R. Kertzer, Ltd.

BLACKBERRY RIDGE WOOLEN MILL, INC.
3776 Forshaug Rd.
Mt. Horeb, WI 53572
www.blackberry-ridge.com

CASCADE YARNS
1224 Andover Park East
Tukwila, WA 98188
www.cascadeyarns.com

CLASSIC ELITE YARNS
300 Jackson St.
Lowell, MA 01852

CRYSTAL PALACE YARNS
160 23rd St.
Richmond, CA 94804
www.straw.com/cpy

DEVON YARNS
1208 Ridge Rd.
Raleigh, NC 27607
www.great-yarns.com

GREEN MOUNTAIN SPINNERY
Box 568
Putney, VT 05346
www.spinnery.com

HABU TEXTILES
135 W. 29th St., Ste. 804
New York, NY 10001
www.habutextiles.com

JCA INC./REYNOLDS/ ARTFUL YARNS
35 Scales Ln.
Townsend, MA 01469-1094

JO SHARP
PO Box 1018
Fremantle, WA 6959 Australia
www.josharp.com.au

KARABELLA
1201 Broadway
New York, NY 10001
www.karabellayarns.com

KNITTING FEVER INC./DEBBIE BLISS
35 Debevoise Ave.
Roosevelt, NY 11575
www.knittingfever.com
In Canada: Diamond Yarn

LA LANA WOOLS
136-C Paseo Norte
Taos, NM 87571
www.lalanawools.com

LOUET SALES
PO Box 267
Ogdensburg, NY 13669
www.louet.com

MAINE MERINO
327 Patten Pond Rd.
Surry, ME 04684
www.mainemerino.com

MUENCH YARNS, INC./GGH
285 Bel Marin Keys Blvd., Unit J
Novato, CA 94949-5763
www.muenchyarns.com
In Canada: Le Fils Muench

TAHKI STACY CHARLES
8000 Cooper Ave., Bldg. 1
Glendale, NY 11385
www.tahkistacycharles.com

UNICORN BOOKS & CRAFTS, INC./JAMIESON'S
1338 Ross St.
Petaluma, CA 94954
www.unicornbooks.com

UNIQUE KOLOURS
28 N. Bacton Hill Rd.
Malvern, PA 19355
www.uniquekolours.com

WESTMINSTER FIBERS/ROWAN
5 Northern Blvd., Ste. 3
Amherst, NH 03031-2335
www.rowanyarns.co.uk
In Canada: Diamond Yarn

CANADIAN SOURCES

DIAMOND YARN OF CANADA LTD.

155 Martin Ross
North York, ON M3J 2L9

FILS DIAMOND DU CANADA LTÉE-DIAMOND YARNS OF CANADA LTD.

9697 Laurent Street
Montréal, QC H3L 2N1
www.diamondyarn.com

LES FILS MUENCH

5640 Rue Valcourt
Brossard, QC J4W 1C5
www.muenchyarns.com

LOUET SALES

RR#4
Prescott, ON K0E 1T0

MISSION FALLS

PO Box 224
Consecon, ON K0K 1T0
www.missionfalls.com

S.R. KERTZER, LTD.

105A Winges Rd.
Woodbridge, ON L4L 6C2
www.kertzer.com